Mindful Magic for the Holiday Witch

A Guide to Winter Solstice, Yule Rituals, Self-Care, and Holiday Healing

Kelsey Pearce

Contents

Preface

Hi, thank you for purchasing this book.

This book is a little from the other **Mindful Magic** books. **Mindful Magic for the Holiday Witch** has a greater focus on managing the holiday season and self-care. There is less reference material for spell crafting than some of my other work. But there are still rituals, recipes, and crafts with magical intention.

Despite some general differences, the same concept exists;

- Magic can be inclusive and accessible

- Practitioners should be approach magic with a sustainability mindset

- We should be aware of cultural appropriation and approach our spell casting with respect.

- No one has to do it all. Embrace what you want. Have fun!

I hope you enjoy. Have a happy and healthy holiday season.

Kelsey

Introduction

EMBRACING THE SEASON OF MINDFUL MAGIC

The winter solstice marks the longest night and the shortest day of the year, a time when the world is wrapped in a hushed blanket of stillness and the magic of Yule is at its peak. This period of introspection and renewal provides an opportunity to look within and reconnect with the rhythms of nature. In this book, we invite you to embark on a journey of mindful magic—a blend of mindfulness practices and witchcraft that helps you find balance, peace, and purpose during the holiday season.

The holiday season is a magical time of year. Late December marks Yule, the Norther Hemisphere Winter Solstice, Hanukkah, Christmas, and Kwanzaa. For the Southern Hemisphere they are experiencing the Summer Solstice. I am fortunate enough to live in an area that experiences snow and there is no denying the magical feeling when the world outside our windows is covered in a blanket of white, or the patterns of frost on windows. Now, don't get me wrong, there is little magical about shoveling driveways, chipping ice off windshields, or dealing with the crowds of people flocking to stores.

What is Mindful Magic?

Mindful magic is the harmonious fusion of mindfulness and witchcraft. It involves being fully present and aware in the moment while incorporating magical practices to enhance your well-being and spiritual connection. During the holiday season, mindful magic can be a powerful tool to help you navigate the complexities and demands of this time of year. By combining the ancient wisdom of witchcraft with modern mindfulness techniques, you can create a holiday season that is meaningful, nurturing, and aligned with your true self.

Purpose of the Book

The goal of this book is to provide you with practical tools and rituals to help you find peace, connection, and purpose amidst the hustle and bustle of the holiday season. We understand that the holidays can be a time of joy and celebration, but they can also bring stress, overwhelm, and emotional challenges. Through mindful magic, we aim to offer you a sanctuary of calm and clarity, allowing you to:

Manage Holiday Stress and Overwhelm: Learn how to slow down, manage your time, and reconnect with your own needs and well-being. The book provides techniques to help you cope with the pressures of shopping, cooking, hosting, and maintaining family traditions.

Address Mental Health Struggles: Discover how to use witchcraft, mindfulness, and ritual to manage feelings of loneliness, depression, grief, or anxiety. Incorporating self-care rituals and mindfulness practices can foster healing, emotional balance, and a sense of inner peace.

Reconnect with Seasonal Traditions: Explore alternative ways to celebrate the holidays that resonate with you on a deeper, personal level. By using witchcraft and pagan-inspired traditions, you can reconnect with the true spirit of Yule and create meaningful rituals.

Balance Giving and Receiving: Embrace the concept of balanced giving—both to others and to yourself. The book encourages self-reflection, self-compassion, and nurturing practices amidst the giving spirit of the season.

Connect with Nature and the Seasons: Reintroduce yourself to the ancient practices that honour the solstice and the changing of the seasons. Use nature-based rituals to ground and centre yourself, tuning into the energies of winter.

Set Boundaries and Manage Social Expectations: Learn tools to set boundaries, practice mindfulness, and recognize when to say "no." Embrace your personal needs and engage with the season in a way that aligns with your emotional capacity.

Create Personal Meaning and Spiritual Fulfilment: Weave witchcraft, spirituality, and personal rituals into your holiday celebrations to create a sense of fulfilment and deeper connection to the season. Focus on the introspective, magical, and self-reflective aspects of the holidays.

By integrating mindful magic into your holiday season, you can transform this time of year into a period of renewal, introspection, and healing. Embrace the quiet stillness of winter, honour the solstice, and create a holiday season that nourishes your soul. Let this book be your guide to mindful magic and holiday healing.

Chapter 1

THE SPIRIT OF THE CHRISTMAS WITCH

The Christmas Witch in Folklore

The Christmas season has always been rich with traditions, myths, and figures, each adding to its magical atmosphere. Amid stories of jolly figures like Santa Claus, there lies another—lesser-known but equally enchanting—the Christmas Witch. She is known by many names and appears in folklore around the world, embodying wisdom, kindness, and a deep-rooted generosity.

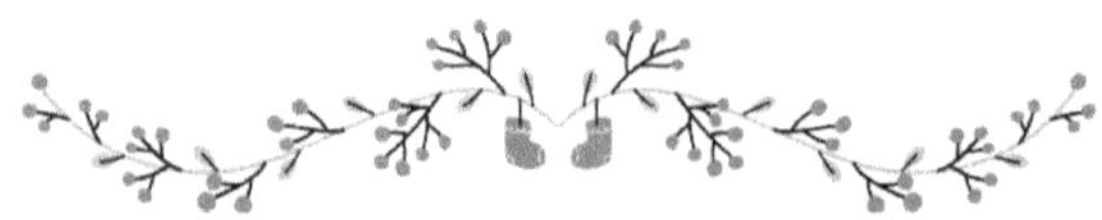

La Befana: The Italian Christmas Witch

One of the most well-known Christmas witches is La Befana, from Italian folklore. According to legend, La Befana was an old woman who spent her days sweeping her modest cottage. When the Three Wise Men passed through her village on their way to visit the Christ child, they invited her to join them. La Befana declined, saying she was too busy with her chores. Later, she regretted not going with them and set off on her own, bringing gifts in search of the newborn king. Although she never found him, she continues her journey each year, visiting children on the night of January 5th, leaving gifts and treats for those who have been good.

La Befana represents both a mother figure and a wise, magical woman of the forest. Her story teaches us about generosity, devotion, and that even in simple, everyday tasks, there lies a kind of magic. Her character invites us to look beyond traditional images of the holiday and see the season as a time for introspection and giving, not just for receiving.

The Yule Witch: A Symbol of Transformation

In Northern Europe, tales of the Yule Witch or "Mother Winter" intertwine with the ancient celebrations of Yule, a festival marking the winter solstice. The Yule Witch was seen as a mysterious, sometimes solitary figure who roamed the countryside during winter, often depicted as an old woman with keen insight and power. She represented the transition from the darkest days into light, symbolizing hope, rebirth, and the transformative power of nature.

The Yule Witch encouraged people to be generous to those less fortunate and to welcome the new year with a heart open to change. Her spirit lives on in modern Yule celebrations and reminds us of the importance of renewal, embracing winter's quiet wisdom, and honouring the cyclical nature of life.

Modern Interpretations of the Christmas Witch

Today, the concept of the Christmas Witch has evolved, blending folklore with modern practices. Many people see the Christmas Witch as a symbol of self-care, empathy, and magic during the holiday season, embodying the qualities we often crave most at this time of year.

Kindness as Magic

The Christmas Witch reminds us that kindness is a magical force. This time of year can be overwhelming, filled with obligations and societal pressures. By choosing small acts of kindness—whether giving a warm smile to a stranger or donating to a local charity—one can embody the spirit of the Christmas Witch. Each thoughtful gesture is like casting a spell of warmth, connection, and compassion.

Creating a Warm, Sacred Space

The Christmas Witch reminds us that our homes can be sanctuaries of peace and comfort. Light candles infuse the air with seasonal scents like pine, cedar, or cloves, and decorate with natural elements such as holly and evergreen wreaths to invite the magic of Yule indoors. Creating a cozy, inviting environment helps to foster a sense of grounding and belonging during the hectic holiday season.

Finding Balance and Self-Care During the Holidays

The holiday season, while full of joy, can also bring emotional challenges, from stress and loneliness to burnout. The 'giving' season includes giving to yourself. There are some negative stereotypes that self-care is equal to indulgence, but genuine self-care is a far cry from indulgent. Self-care should include checking in on your physical, mental, and spiritual well-being (spirituality does not refer to only religion, rather, your core beliefs and values). The holidays can take a physical toll on us and we should make sure that aches and pains are being addressed. Our bodies are nourished in the hustle and bustle.

Managing Mental Health Struggles

The holiday season can intensify feelings of loneliness, anxiety, or depression.

Seasonal Affective Disorder (SAD) is a type of depression that occurs at certain times of the year, typically in the winter months. The exact cause of SAD is not fully understood, but it is believed to be linked to reduced exposure to sunlight, which can affect serotonin levels (a neurotransmitter involved in mood regulation), melatonin levels (which regulate sleep patterns), and the body's internal clock (circadian rhythm). If you are at a higher risk of SAD (previous depression, family history, living further away from the equator) you should be extra-aware of the potential influence the season could have on your mood.

I have found that often times in the happiest moments of the holidays; I am over-come with sadness. I grieve for those I have lost that are missing from festivities. Sometimes the reality of the situation does not align with what I had expected, and I am washed with a profound sense of disappointment. If you have every painstakingly wrapped presents for hours with pretty bows only to have your kids rip through them in a matter of minutes and ask if there is any more, you know the feeling.

If you're experiencing these challenges, take time to practice self-compassion and prioritize your mental health. Set aside time each day for quiet moments or meditation. Mindfulness exercises, such as deep breathing or journaling, can help you stay present and grounded, easing feelings of overwhelm.

Connecting with Nature and the Seasons

In winter, it's easy to feel detached from the natural world. Reconnect with the Yule Witch's spirit by embracing the quiet beauty of this season. Go for nature walks and observe the winter landscape, noting the resilience of life even in the dormant trees and the crisp air. Collect small tokens of nature—a pinecone, a smooth stone—and bring them indoors to add a natural touch to your decor and rituals.

Incorporating Nature into Rituals: Create a small altar with natural winter el-ements like evergreen branches, pinecones, or holly. This can serve as a daily reminder of the cycles of life and nature's resilience. Take time to appreciate these elements, letting them help you feel more in tune with the season.

Setting Boundaries and Managing Social Expectations

The holiday season often comes with increased social obligations, which can lead to burnout and emotional fatigue. The Christmas Witch teaches us to prioritize well-being over social expectations. Set boundaries around your time and energy, giving yourself permission to say "no" when needed.

Remember that you don't have to meet every holiday expectation. It's okay to decline invitations or take a break from gatherings if you're feeling overwhelmed. Prioritize activities that align with your values and make you feel nourished.

Finding Your Own Inner Christmas Witch

Embracing the spirit of the Christmas Witch doesn't mean you need a broomstick or magical cauldron. Instead, it's about connecting to the core qualities of these legendary figures—wisdom, warmth, and generosity—and embodying them in your own way. Here are a few ways to find and express your inner Christmas Witch:

Practice Compassion and Patience

During the holiday rush, take moments to slow down and be present. Like La Befana, be mindful in your actions and interactions. Approach others with understanding and patience, offering kindness even when tensions run high. This mindful approach to life mirrors the wisdom of the Christmas Witch, who knows the power of slowing down to reflect on what really matters.

Cultivate a Ritual of Generosity

Try adding a ritual of giving to your holiday season. This could be as simple as baking treats for friends, leaving a secret note of encouragement for a coworker, or creating small gifts with intention. Consider giving something meaningful that aligns with the values of the Christmas Witch—something that adds magic to another's life or provides comfort.

Nurture Inner Peace Through Reflection

Find moments to step back from the holiday bustle and nurture your inner peace. Light a candle at night and sit quietly, setting intentions for yourself and others. Reflect on the lessons of the past year and the ways you've grown, just as the Yule Witch teaches us to embrace cycles of change. This practice can help you stay centred and connected to the magic within.

Create Your Own Holiday Rituals

In addition to traditional customs, try creating a few new rituals of your own. You might create an altar for the season, perhaps with a pine bough, a red candle for warmth, and a crystal like smoky quartz for grounding. Or, take a walk in nature and collect small tokens to add to your space. These small acts honour the spirit of the Yule Witch, who finds magic in the earth and its seasonal rhythms.

By looking to the figures like La Befana and the Yule Witch, we find that the Christmas Witch isn't bound to any one tradition; she's a spirit of warmth, introspection, and quiet magic that we can all embody. As you go through the holiday season, remember that the spirit of the Christmas Witch lives in each act of kindness, each moment of reflection, and each offering of warmth you give.

Embrace the wisdom of the Christmas Witch and let her spirit guide you through this season, finding balance, joy, and a touch of magic in every day.

Chapter 2

SETTING INTENTIONS FOR THE YULE SEASON

The Yule season brings with it an invitation to slow down, reflect, and approach the holidays with mindful intention. Amid celebrations, gatherings, and traditions, it's easy to become swept up in the whirlwind of the season. By setting intentions for Yule, we can create a holiday experience that aligns with our core desires, allowing us to celebrate with purpose, joy, and a touch of magic.

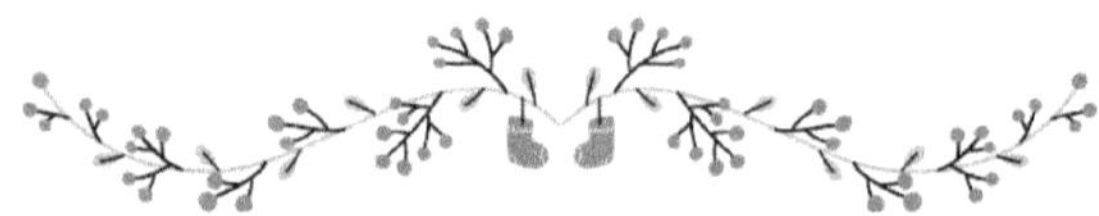

Holiday Intentions and Reflection

Setting intentions for the holiday season starts with grounding yourself in your own values, reflecting on what matters to you, and envisioning the Yule season as you most wish to experience it. When you connect with what you want to feel, create, and share, you open the door to a more meaningful holiday, allowing yourself to celebrate in a way that resonates deeply with your soul.

Acknowledging Mental Health Struggles

The holiday season can bring a range of emotions, and for some, it's a time marked by feelings of loneliness, anxiety, or even depression. If you find yourself struggling, remember that it's okay to feel this way and that you're not alone. Consider incorporating simple self-care rituals to help ground and uplift your spirit, like journaling, gentle movement, or practicing gratitude for small moments of joy. Mindfulness exercises, such as deep breathing or grounding techniques, can also bring calm during anxious moments, helping you stay present and connected to your inner peace.

Guided Visualization: Your Ideal Holiday Experience

Start with a guided visualization exercise to help centre your thoughts and clarify your holiday intentions. Find a quiet, comfortable place where you can sit undisturbed for a few minutes, perhaps lighting a candle or burning a soothing incense to set the mood. Close your eyes, take a deep breath, and begin to visualize the Yule season you desire.

Imagine your surroundings: Picture your ideal holiday space. Is it warmly lit, filled with the scent of pine and spices, decorated with touches of red, green, and gold? Envision the details that bring you comfort and joy.

Feel the energy you want to cultivate: Are you surrounded by loved ones, sharing laughter and warmth? Or perhaps you're enjoying quiet, peaceful solitude, reflecting on the year past. Visualize how you want to feel—whether it's calm, joyful, connected, or renewed.

Focus on specific experiences: Picture a few special moments you hope to create during this season. Maybe it's a heartfelt conversation, a shared meal, or a personal ritual of gratitude. Allow yourself to embrace the positive emotions tied to these moments.

Bring awareness to your senses: What sounds, scents, and tastes make the holiday magical for you? Perhaps it's the sound of a crackling fire, the scent of cinnamon, or the taste of spiced tea. Picture yourself immersed in these elements, allowing them to ground you in the present.

When you open your eyes, take a moment to reflect on your visualization. You might jot down any thoughts or images that came to mind. This visualization can help clarify what you most want to experience during the Yule season, setting a sound foundation for your holiday intentions.

Creating Intention Cards

With your holiday intentions clearer, you can bring them into daily focus by making Intention Cards—small, personalized reminders that capture your aspirations for the season. These cards can serve as gentle guides, encouraging you to stay connected to your values even amidst the hustle and bustle of the holidays.

Select your materials: You'll need some small, sturdy cards or pieces of paper (recycled holiday cards work well for this) and any art supplies you like, such as markers, paints, or coloured pencils.

Write your intentions: On each card, write an intention or affirmation that resonates with you for the holiday season. These could be simple phrases like "Embrace joy," "Practice patience," "Connect deeply," or "Savour moments of peace." Feel free to get creative and specific—whatever reflects your unique holiday wishes.

Decorate the cards: Add colours, symbols, or small illustrations that feel meaningful to you. Reds, greens, and golds can symbolize warmth and abundance, while blues and silvers can represent peace and introspection. Perhaps you add a small pentacle for protection, or a sprig of holly for strength and resilience.

Place them around your space: Display the cards throughout your home, where you'll see them often—on your mirror, beside your bed, at your desk, or on your altar. Let each card act as a subtle reminder to align your actions and energy with your true intentions for the season.

Creating these Intention Cards is a simple yet powerful way to infuse each day of Yule with meaning, connecting you to the deeper purpose of your celebrations.

Managing Emotional Fatigue and Burnout

The holidays can bring unique social pressures and expectations. If you're feeling overwhelmed, it's important to prioritize your emotional well-being and set boundaries. Politely declining invitations or scheduling time for yourself are acts of self-compassion, not selfishness. Take moments to check in with yourself and honour your needs—even if it means saying "no" or carving out quiet time. By balancing your social engagements, you'll have more energy to fully enjoy the moments that matter most.

Building a Holiday Manifesto

Once you have a sense of your intentions, it can be helpful to bring them together in a Holiday Manifesto—a personal declaration of what you wish this season to embody. Your manifesto is a guiding statement, a reminder of the qualities and experiences you value most during the holidays.

Crafting Your Holiday Manifesto

Reflect on your values: Start by jotting down a list of words or phrases that represent what you want this season to be about. Think beyond material things or traditional expectations; instead, focus on what brings you true fulfilment. Your values might include simplicity, connection, creativity, gratitude, or generosity.

Identify your core desires: Consider what you want to experience, feel, and achieve during Yule. Do you want to feel closer to family, make time for solitude, or give back to your community? Write down these desires and allow yourself to be honest and open.

Set clear, realistic intentions: With your values and desires in mind, set specific intentions that will help you create the season you envision. These could be small practices, such as "light a candle each night for gratitude," or broader goals like "spend time in nature weekly to ground myself." Make sure your intentions feel achievable, so they add to your joy rather than stress.

Write your manifesto: Bring these elements together into a short, heartfelt statement. Your Holiday Manifesto might look like this:

"This Yule, I will embrace simplicity and warmth. I will connect deeply with those I love and give myself permission to rest and reflect. I will savour small moments of joy and find peace in the quiet magic of winter."

Display your manifesto: Place it somewhere you'll see it often—near your intention cards, on your altar, or tucked into a journal. Let your manifesto be a steady reminder of the Yule experience you're choosing to create, helping you stay grounded and true to yourself throughout the holiday.

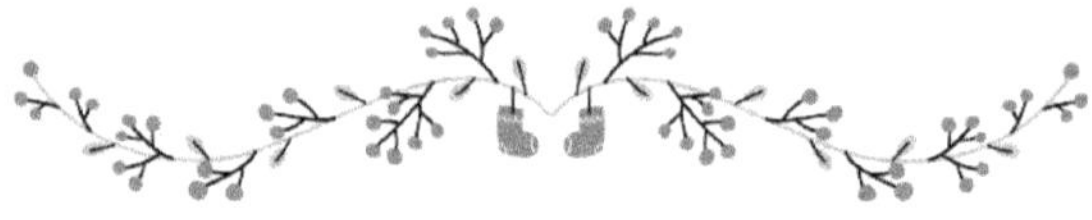

Setting intentions and crafting a Holiday Manifesto offer powerful ways to approach Yule with clarity, kindness, and purpose. As you move through the season, allow these practices to centre you, reconnecting you to the beauty and magic of winter. Whether in the quiet glow of a candle, the warmth of a gathering, or a moment of peace by yourself, each day of Yule can be infused with intention, making this season yours.

Embrace the magic of mindful celebration, and let this Yule be a season that nurtures your spirit, fills your heart, and inspires your path forward.

Chapter 3

HOLIDAY CRYSTALS FOR STRESS AND RENEWAL

The holiday season, while joyful, can also bring a unique set of challenges. From managing holiday gatherings to balancing personal responsibilities, it's common to feel stress and fatigue during these busy winter months. This chapter introduces the soothing power of crystals to help bring calm, renewal, and balance. By incorporating crystal energy into your daily routine, you can cultivate a peaceful and resilient spirit throughout the season. We'll explore crystals for stress relief, stones for renewed energy, and the art of creating a holiday crystal grid to infuse your space with harmonious energy. Additionally, you'll find ways to reconnect with seasonal traditions, incorporate nature, and support emotional well-being.

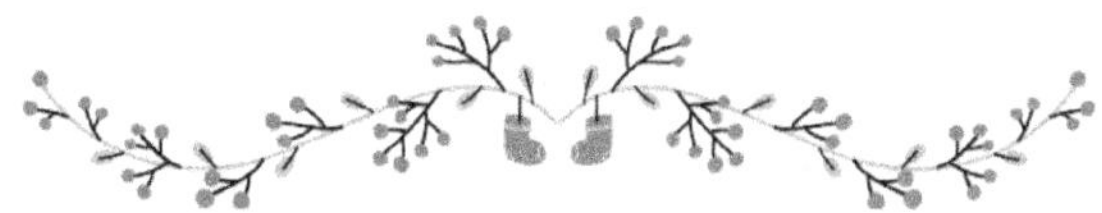

Crystals for Stress Relief

The holidays are a time of celebration but can easily become overwhelming. These crystals are known for their calming properties and can help balance emotions and reduce stress. Consider carrying one with you, placing it in your home, or holding it during a mindful moment of deep breathing.

Amethyst: Known as the "Stone of Serenity," amethyst is a popular choice for stress relief. Its calming energy can help ease anxious thoughts and bring a sense of tranquillity during busy days. To use amethyst for relaxation, hold it in your hand during meditation or keep it nearby when you need a calming influence.

Use it for: Calming the mind, supporting relaxation, encouraging restful sleep.

Best placements: Beside your bed, in a calming corner of your home, or on your desk for focus.

Rose Quartz: This gentle pink stone, often called the "Stone of Love," not only promotes self-love but also encourages emotional balance. Rose quartz can help soothe the heart and mind during tense situations, reminding you to approach challenges with compassion.

Use it for: Emotional balance, stress relief, cultivating compassion.

Best placements: Near the heart (in a necklace or pocket), or in areas where you seek peace, like a meditation or reading space.

Black Tourmaline: Black tourmaline is a powerful stone for grounding and protection, which can be especially useful when you're feeling drained or overwhelmed by holiday activities. Its stabilizing energy shields against negative influences, providing support when you need a grounding influence.

Use it for: Protection, grounding, dispelling negative energy.

Best placements: Near entryways, in rooms where gatherings are held, or on your person for a sense of security.

Crystals for Renewed Energy

As the days grow shorter and the holiday to-do list grows longer, it's natural to feel fatigued. These crystals can help boost joy, renew vitality, and promote positivity, helping you maintain a joyful spirit and sense of well-being.

Citrine: Known as the "Stone of Abundance," citrine is celebrated for its ability to uplift and energize. Its warm, golden colour brings a touch of sunlight into the winter months, inspiring joy and positivity. Citrine is also believed to support personal empowerment and clarity, helping you move through holiday tasks with confidence.

Use it for: Joy, motivation, personal empowerment.

Best placements: In a sunny spot, near workspaces, or in a living room to share its warmth with others.

Clear Quartz: Clear quartz is a versatile crystal that amplifies positive energy and promotes mental clarity. When you're feeling overwhelmed, this crystal can help bring focus, clearing away holiday clutter and keeping you aligned with your intentions.

Use it for: Amplifying positive energy, mental clarity, promoting focus.

Best placements: Anywhere you want to enhance clarity, such as on your desk or near your holiday grimoire.

Carnelian: This vibrant, red-orange stone is known as the "Stone of Vitality." Carnelian stimulates creativity and enthusiasm, making it a wonderful choice for embracing the warmth and excitement of the holiday season. It's especially helpful if you need a little extra motivation or joy as you complete holiday preparations.

Use it for: Vitality, creativity, enthusiasm.

Best placements: In spaces where you create or gather, like a kitchen or living room, or near holiday crafting materials for inspiration.

Creating a Crystal Holiday Grid

A crystal grid is a powerful tool for enhancing the energy of a space. During the holidays, you can create a crystal grid intending to bring peace, harmony, and joy into your home. By arranging selected crystals in a specific pattern, you can amplify their effects and create a calming atmosphere, whether for family gatherings or quiet moments.

Setting Up Your Crystal Grid

Choose Your Intention: Decide on the main focus for your grid. Are you seeking calm and harmony for gatherings, a peaceful environment for self-reflection, or protection against stress? Set a clear intention for your grid.

Select Your Crystals: Based on your intention, choose stones that align with your goals.

- For peace and harmony: Amethyst, rose quartz, and clear quartz.

- For joy and positivity: Citrine, carnelian, and clear quartz.

- For grounding and protection: Black tourmaline and rose quartz.

Incorporate Seasonal Traditions

Consider weaving in elements of Yule, such as traditional holiday crystals like garnet for warmth or green aventurine for good fortune. Including these traditional stones can create a sense of connection to seasonal customs.

Arrange Your Grid

Centre Stone: Start by placing a crystal in the centre of your grid that represents the core of your intention. Clear quartz works well as a central stone for amplifying energy, or you may choose amethyst for calm or citrine for joy.

Supporting Stones: Arrange additional crystals around the centre stone in a pattern that feels balanced. You can create a circle, triangle, or any shape that feels intuitive. Symmetry is often soothing, so consider placing crystals equidistantly around the centre.

Activate the Grid: Once arranged, sit quietly by your grid, close your eyes, and envision your intention filling the space. Touch each crystal lightly, imagining a current of energy linking each stone together in harmony.

Display Your Grid: Keep your crystal grid somewhere that aligns with your intention, such as a central room in the home, near your holiday altar, or in a private space for personal reflection. Allow its energy to support you throughout the season.

Connecting with Nature and Setting Boundaries

To deepen your connection to nature and set personal boundaries during this busy season, you might create an outdoor grid or use stones found in nature, like river rocks, to ground the grid. To support self-care, set up your grid in a dedicated space where you can retreat for moments of calm. Crystals like rose quartz and amethyst can help with emotional boundaries, reminding you to prioritize self-care over social pressures.

Balancing Giving and Receiving

The holiday season is also a time of giving. You might consider creating small, personalized crystal grids as gifts for loved ones, sharing the balance of giving and receiving through the joy of crystal energy. Whether it's a single stone or a miniature grid, gifting crystals with intention can bring a meaningful connection to those around you.

This chapter offers a gentle guide to working with crystals as a way to cultivate peace, renewal, and balance during the holidays. Whether you're new to crystals or looking to deepen your practice, remember that each stone is a tool to help you connect with your own inner peace and joy. Embrace their presence as allies on your path to a mindful, magical holiday season.

Chapter 4

HOLIDAY ANIMALS AND THEIR SIGNIFICANCE

In winter holiday traditions, animals like deer, owls, bears, and cardinals are more than symbols of the season; they're powerful archetypes that carry unique energies and lessons. Each animal embodies specific qualities that align with the themes of Yule and Christmas, offering guidance, protection, and insight for the season. By understanding their magical meanings and incorporating their symbolism into our rituals, we can strengthen our connection to nature, enhance our self-care practices, and find inspiration in their unique wisdom.

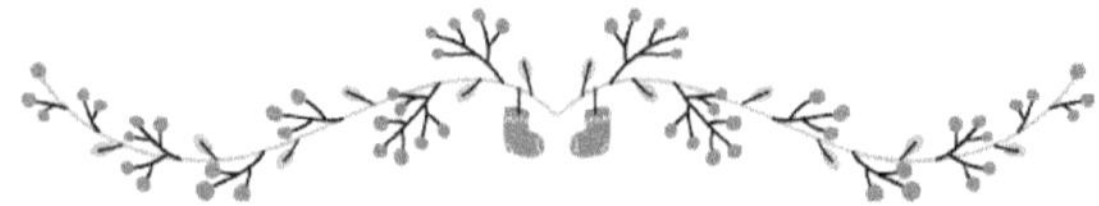

Holiday Stress and Overwhelm

The holiday season, while joyful, can also bring about stress and overwhelm. By tapping into the energies of these animals, we can find support in managing the season's challenges. For instance, the bear's energy encourages us to set boundaries and honour our need for rest, while deer energy reminds us to find calm amidst the holiday chaos.

Mental Health Struggles During the Holidays

Many experience heightened mental health struggles during the holidays. The qualities of these animals can serve as emotional anchors. The owl's wisdom, for example, can offer clarity and introspection, helping us find solace in quiet moments. Embracing these animal energies can foster emotional resilience and support mental well-being.

Deer—Grace and Renewal

The deer is often associated with Yule, symbolizing gentleness, resilience, and the journey through darkness toward the returning light. Deer, especially reindeer, are depicted in various holiday traditions, embodying the energy of winter as they gracefully navigate snowy forests.

Magical Meaning: The deer teaches us to embrace resilience with gentleness, embodying quiet strength even during challenging times. As winter reaches its peak, the deer reminds us that the light will soon return.

Qualities: Grace, renewal, patience, inner peace.

Ways to Connect with Deer Energy:

Visualization Exercise: Imagine yourself walking through a serene, snowy forest as a deer would—calm, alert, and mindful. Focus on embodying their gentle grace throughout your holiday season.

Symbolic Décor: Place deer ornaments or artwork in your home as a reminder to move through each day with calm resilience.

Affirmation: "I embrace the quiet strength within me, welcoming peace and renewal."

Owl—Wisdom and Introspection

Owls are symbols of wisdom, insight, and mystery, making them ideal companions for the introspective energy of Yule. Known for their nocturnal nature, owls encourage us to look inward, listen to our intuition, and trust our inner voice during the reflective holiday season.

Magical Meaning: Owls guide us toward self-reflection and introspection, helping us see clearly even in darkness. They represent the wisdom we gain from looking within.

Qualities: Insight, intuition, clarity, introspection.

Ways to Connect with Owl Energy:

Nighttime Journaling: Dedicate time in the evenings to journal by candlelight, reflecting on the day's experiences and any personal insights. Owls inspire this quiet, introspective practice.

Winter Solstice Meditation: On the longest night, meditate with owl imagery, contemplating the wisdom hidden within your own thoughts and experiences.

Affirmation: "I trust the wisdom within me and embrace the clarity that comes from self-reflection."

Bear—Strength and Protection

The bear, known for hibernating through winter, symbolizes rest, resilience, and the power of personal boundaries. Bears remind us to protect our energy, take time for rest, and emerge renewed when the time is right.

Magical Meaning: Bears encourage us to prioritize self-care, honour our need for rest, and create protective boundaries during the busyness of the holiday season.

Qualities: Strength, grounding, self-care, protection.

Ways to Connect with Bear Energy:

Hibernation Ritual: Set aside a day during the holiday season for complete rest, allowing yourself to recharge without obligations. Think of it as a mini-hibernation for mental and emotional renewal.

Protective Charm: Create a small bear charm or talisman to carry with you or keep in your home, symbolizing personal boundaries and self-care.

Affirmation: "I honour my need for rest and protect my energy, nurturing my inner strength."

Balancing Giving and Receiving

In the spirit of giving, we may sometimes overextend ourselves. Using animal energies to foster balance can help. For example, creating small, animal-themed charms or decorations to share with loved ones offers a heartfelt, symbolic way to gift without overburdening yourself. These charms can embody the qualities of your chosen animal, like the bear for protection or the deer for peace, creating a sense of balance in giving and receiving.

Cardinal—Hope and Vitality

The cardinal, with its striking red plumage, is often associated with vitality, warmth, and the beauty of persistence through winter's chill. Cardinals are seen as messengers of hope, embodying the strength to endure the cold and the promise of renewal.

Magical Meaning: Cardinals represent resilience, joy, and the warmth of hope in dark times. Their bright red feathers symbolize courage and a zest for life, reminding us to carry positivity through the season.

Qualities: Hope, vitality, resilience, courage.

Ways to Connect with Cardinal Energy:

Morning Affirmation: Start each day with an affirmation inspired by the cardinal's message of hope and vitality, encouraging you to embrace each day with courage and warmth.

Cardinal Symbolism: Place a cardinal ornament or artwork in your home to remind you of the beauty and resilience within, and the promise of new beginnings.

Affirmation: "I carry hope and courage through winter's chill, embracing life with joy and strength."

Connecting to Nature and the Seasons

To deepen your connection with these animal energies, spend time in natural environments that reflect their habitats. Observe deer in nature if possible, or create bird feeders for cardinals, inviting their presence and energy into your surroundings. Simple acts like these ground us in the season and foster a deeper relationship with the animals.

Fox—Adaptability and Cleverness

The fox is often associated with adaptability, cleverness, and playfulness, qualities that can help us navigate the social dynamics of the holiday season. As creatures known for their cunning and resilience, foxes encourage us to approach holiday gatherings and seasonal challenges with creativity and wit.

Magical Meaning: Foxes embody adaptability, reminding us to stay lighthearted and resourceful during the holiday season. They teach us to find joy and creativity, even in unexpected situations.

Qualities: Adaptability, cleverness, playfulness, resilience.

Ways to Connect with Fox Energy:

Creative Ritual: Bring fox energy into your daily life by trying new approaches to old routines. Change up your holiday decorations, or try a new recipe, allowing adaptability and creativity to lead.

Fox Ornament: Place a fox ornament in your home as a reminder to stay lighthearted, even when navigating challenges.

Affirmation: "I move through change with resilience and creativity, embracing the unexpected with joy."

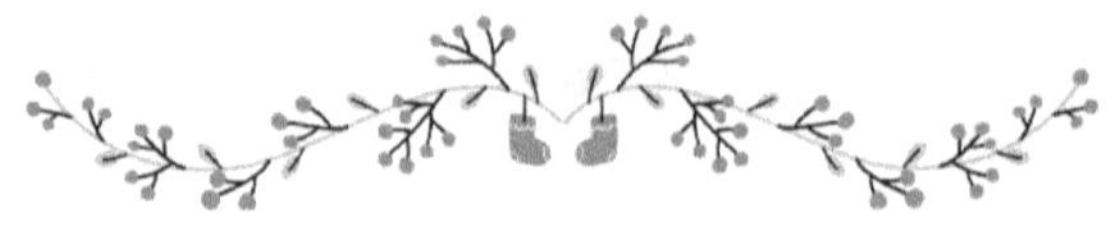

By incorporating these animal energies, you can draw on their unique strengths and qualities for a more meaningful Yule. Let their archetypal energies guide you in creating a season filled with wisdom, grace, hope, and resilience, offering support for managing holiday stress, reconnecting with nature, and embracing the season with balance and joy.

Chapter 5

THE MAGICAL SIGNIFICANCE OF YULE AND CHRISTMAS COLOURS

In the Yule and Christmas season, colours aren't just decorative—they're full of ancient symbolism and magical energy. By aligning with the colours of the season, you can bring the spirit of Yule into your home, creating a space that feels both festive and filled with intention. In this chapter, we'll explore the traditional colours of Yule, their meanings, and ways to use them in your holiday decor and rituals.

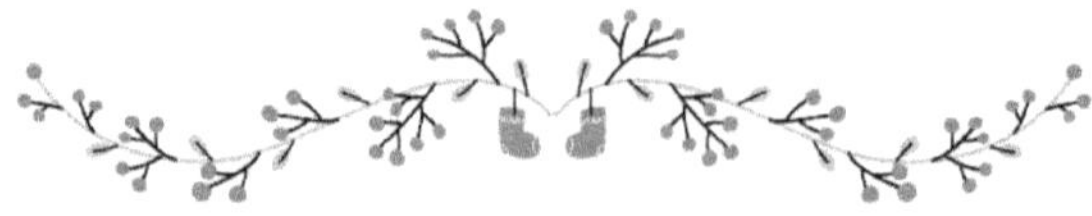

Traditional Colours and Their Meanings

Each classic holiday colour carries a unique energy and symbolism in witchcraft and folklore. Here's a look at the traditional colours of the season and the magic they hold:

Red: Often associated with protection, passion, and courage. Red's fiery energy is ideal for adding warmth to cold winter days and creating a protective aura around the home. This colour also symbolizes love and vitality, reminding us of the strength and warmth we share with loved ones.

Green: Representing abundance, growth, and renewal, green is a reminder of the evergreen trees that persist through winter, symbolizing the promise of rebirth. It's also a colour of prosperity, making it ideal for attracting good fortune and abundance into the new year.

Gold: Gold embodies prosperity, success, and the return of the sun. During Yule, it's a powerful colour to honour the rebirth of the sun after the winter solstice. This bright, joyful colour is perfect for setting intentions of success, wealth, and optimism for the coming year.

White: Symbolizing purity, peace, and clarity, white is a cleansing colour that helps create a serene, reflective atmosphere. It's associated with snow, stillness, and the purity of new beginnings, making it a perfect colour for spells of peace and healing.

Silver: Linked to the moon and intuition, silver represents magic, wisdom, and emotional insight. It's an ideal colour for setting intentions of inner guidance and connecting with the softer energies of winter.

Alleviating Holiday Stress and Overwhelm

The holiday season can bring stress and a sense of overwhelm. Incorporating calming colours like white and green into your space can help create a peaceful atmosphere that supports mental and emotional well-being.

Green for Balance and Grounding: Adding greenery through plants, wreaths, or garlands can connect you with nature's calm and grounding energy. Green reminds us to slow down, breathe, and reconnect with ourselves amidst the holiday hustle.

White for Clarity and Calm: Using white candles, linens, or decorative accents can bring a sense of stillness and peace, helping to calm the mind and reduce stress.

Mental Health Support During the Holidays

The introspective energy of winter can bring up emotions that may be challenging during the holiday season. Here's how specific colours can offer support:

Blue for Peace and Comfort: While not a traditional Yule colour, adding blue can help create a soothing environment for reflection. Blue lights, candles, or even ornaments can bring a feeling of calm that supports mental health.

Silver for Introspection and Clarity: Silver's connection to the moon and intuition makes it a perfect colour for journaling or meditation spaces. This colour can help you tap into inner wisdom, providing clarity and perspective during emotional times.

Incorporating Colours into Gift-Giving Practices

Holiday traditions often emphasize giving, which can sometimes create an imbalance between giving and receiving. Using colour symbolism in gift-giving can help bring a sense of mindfulness and intention to the practice:

Red for Protection and Passion: Wrap gifts in red for friends or family members who could use some extra protection or vitality. This thoughtful touch adds a layer of intention that makes the gift even more special.

Green for Growth and Renewal: Use green ribbons or wrapping paper to represent growth, especially if you wish to support someone's new year aspirations or personal growth.

Consider making or gifting charms or decorations that incorporate these colours as a way of sharing the magical energy of the season with loved ones.

Connecting to Nature and the Seasons

Strengthen your bond with the natural world by incorporating natural elements into your colour-themed decor. Seasonal greenery, branches, and flowers not only bring beauty but also deepen your connection to the cycles of the earth:

Evergreens and Pinecones: Green branches symbolize growth and endurance, while pinecones represent the promise of new beginnings. Use them in wreaths or arrangements to honour the resilience of nature through winter.

Winter Berries and Holly: Red berries symbolize vitality and protection. Adding these to your decor celebrates the natural beauty of the season and aligns your space with Yule's magical energy.

Managing Emotional Fatigue and Social Expectations

The holidays often bring social expectations that can lead to emotional fatigue. Setting up personal spaces with intentional colours can help create a refuge for recharging:

White for Reflection and Peace: Set up a cozy corner with white accents, blankets, and soft lighting for a peaceful sanctuary where you can recharge away from the bustle of gatherings. White's clarity and simplicity help clear emotional clutter, supporting calm and focus.

Gold for Positivity and Joy: For a space that uplifts and energizes, incorporate gold through candles, ornaments, or small decor items. Gold's warm glow can help lift your spirits and bring joy when social dynamics feel overwhelming.

Creating a Colourful Yule Altar

A Yule altar can be as simple or elaborate as you like, becoming a beautiful space to hold your intentions for the season. Using the colours of Yule, you can design an altar that resonates with the energies you want to welcome into your life:

Setting Up the Altar: Begin by draping a cloth in one of the season's colours, like green or gold, over a small table or shelf. Add candles, crystals, or personal items in the traditional Yule colours to create a harmonious, intentional display.

Elements of the Altar: Place specific objects to represent each colour's energy. For example:

- A red candle for protection

- Evergreen branches for growth

- A gold ornament or coin for prosperity

- A white stone for peace

- A silver bell for intuition

Daily or Weekly Ritual: Light a candle on your altar each day or week to reinforce your intentions. For instance, you might start with green for growth and abundance, moving to red for protection as the holiday season unfolds.

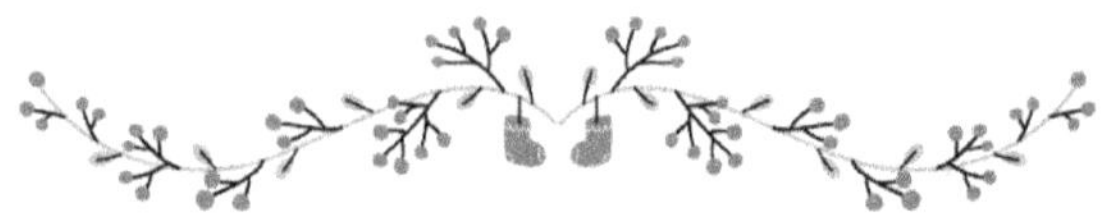

By using colour to fill your holiday season with magic, each hue you incorporate becomes a reminder of the beauty and strength of Yule's energies. From festive decor to personal rituals, the colours of Yule bring more than beauty—they bring a sense of purpose and connection to the magic of the season.

Chapter 6

YULE SYMBOLS AND THEIR TRANSFORMATION IN CHRISTMAS TRADITIONS

Yule, celebrated on the Winter Solstice, marks the shortest day and longest night of the year. This ancient festival not only symbolizes the depth of winter but also celebrates the gradual return of the sun and the promise of spring's rebirth. Many of Yule's traditional symbols—such as the Yule log, holly, mistletoe, and evergreen wreaths—have been carried forward into Christmas celebrations, subtly preserving the ancient wisdom and resilience associated with this season. In this chapter, we'll explore the meanings behind these enduring symbols, how to incorporate them into your own Yule witchcraft practice, and how their energies can support emotional well-being during the holiday season.

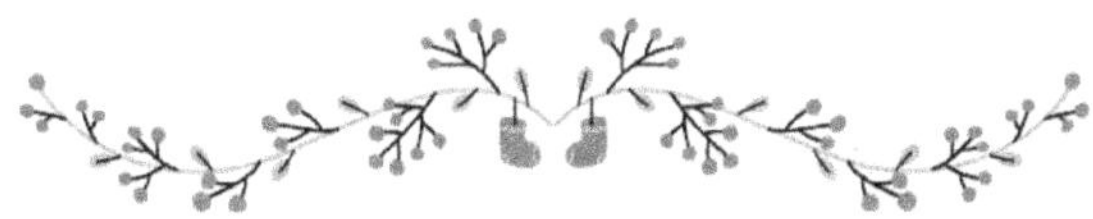

The Significance of Yule and the Winter Solstice

Yule is a time for reflection, gratitude, and honouring the cycles of life. Celebrated around December 21st, the Winter Solstice is when the sun appears at its lowest point, giving us the shortest day and longest night of the year. Ancient cultures viewed this moment as the "birth" of the sun, a time when light would gradually return to the world. Yule is therefore a festival of hope and resilience, reminding us that even in the darkest times, warmth and renewal are on the horizon.

Traditional Yule Symbols and Their Meanings

Each Yule symbol holds specific meanings that resonate with the season's themes of rebirth, endurance, and protection. Here's a closer look at these powerful symbols, how they've shaped modern holiday traditions, and ways to incorporate them into daily practices to support mental and emotional well-being:

The Yule Log

Traditionally, the Yule log was cut from an oak or ash tree, chosen for its strength and protection qualities. Burning the Yule log was a way to ward off negative spirits and bring warmth to the home on the darkest night of the year. Today, the log symbolizes resilience and warmth, and it's often represented as a decorated cake or candle.

Incorporate in Your Practice: Create a Yule log ritual by decorating a log with seasonal greenery and burning it (safely), or substitute it with a Yule log cake or decorated candle on your altar. Focus on letting go of past challenges as you light the log, allowing its warmth to bring a sense of renewal. This practice can also be a calming way to manage holiday stress, encouraging you to release the year's burdens.

Holly

Known for its bright red berries and glossy green leaves, holly is a symbol of protection and vitality. In ancient lore, holly was thought to ward off evil spirits, providing a shield for the home. Its red berries also symbolize the life force that endures through the winter season.

Incorporate in Your Practice: Use holly in your home decor to invite protection and vitality. Hang a sprig on your door or above a window for seasonal magic, or add it to your Yule altar. Holly's protective energy helps create a safe and peaceful environment, which can alleviate stress and provide emotional support during overwhelming holiday moments. Consider making small holly wreaths as gifts for loved ones, fostering a balanced sense of giving and receiving.

Mistletoe

This mystical plant, known as the "kissing plant," has long been associated with peace, love, and protection. In Norse mythology, mistletoe was used to reconcile feuding parties, which is why it became a symbol of peace and love. The tradition of kissing under the mistletoe may have its roots in this idea of harmony and affection.

Incorporate in Your Practice: Hang mistletoe in your home as a symbol of peace and friendship. Create a mistletoe charm bag, or place sprigs around your space to bring harmony into your life. Sharing a moment of gratitude or affection under the mistletoe can bring a sense of comfort, especially for those experiencing mental health struggles during the holidays. Its peaceful energy helps foster connection and calm.

Evergreen Wreaths

Wreaths made from evergreen branches represent eternal life and the cyclical nature of the seasons. In Yule celebrations, the circular shape of the wreath also symbolizes the Wheel of the Year, the ongoing journey through life, death, and rebirth.

Incorporate in Your Practice: Craft your own wreath from evergreen branches and adorn it with symbols of Yule, like pinecones, holly, and ribbon. Hanging it on your door serves as a protective talisman, while creating the wreath itself can be a grounding activity that reconnects you to nature. This simple act of gathering greenery can remind you of your connection to the earth, offering a sense of calm in the face of holiday burnout.

Addressing Holiday Stress, Mental Health, and Social Fatigue

Incorporating Yule symbols into your daily holiday routine can provide relief from the stress, emotional fatigue, and mental health challenges that often accompany this season.

- **Managing Social Expectations**: If social gatherings feel overwhelming, use the meaning of the Yule log as a guide to set boundaries and release the need to meet every expectation. Let the log's energy encourage you to reserve space for rest, helping you prioritize self-care over social obligations.

- **Balancing Giving and Receiving**: Consider incorporating Yule symbols like holly and mistletoe into your gift-giving practices. Handmade gifts such as holly wreaths or mistletoe charms are not only heartfelt but also foster a sense of balance in giving and receiving, connecting you to the intention behind your gifts rather than the pressure of consumerism.

- **Nature Connection for Grounding**: For those experiencing a disconnection from nature, Yule provides opportunities to reconnect with the natural world. Gathering evergreen branches, creating an outdoor Yule altar, or simply spending a few minutes outdoors can help you feel more grounded. Touching the cold bark of trees or inhaling the crisp winter air brings a sensory reminder of nature's resilience, offering strength and support during challenging times.

How Yule Symbols Have Influenced Christmas Traditions

Many Yule symbols were later incorporated into Christmas customs, carrying themes of protection, love, and resilience into holiday celebrations. Here are a few ways these symbols transformed:

- **Yule Log as a Festive Dessert**: The Yule log tradition evolved into the popular "bûche de Noël" cake, a dessert that visually resembles a log and is often decorated with sugared holly leaves or edible glitter to symbolize warmth and abundance.

- **Holly and Mistletoe as Holiday Decor**: Both holly and mistletoe have become popular decorations during the Christmas season, adorning homes, wreaths, and holiday cards. Their inclusion continues the ancient practice of inviting protection, joy, and love into the home.

- **Evergreen Wreaths for Doorways**: While evergreen wreaths were once a pagan symbol, they now welcome the holiday season with added ornaments or lights, symbolizing festivity and goodwill. Even secular Christmas practices embrace this enduring symbol of the natural world.

Incorporating Yule Symbols in Your Witchcraft Practice

These symbols can become powerful components in your Yule rituals, offering support during times of stress, sadness, or fatigue:

Yule Altar with Symbols: Create an altar dedicated to Yule using these symbols to invite in their magic. Place holly for protection, a Yule log or candle for warmth, mistletoe for peace, and a wreath for eternity. Arrange them thoughtfully and add any personal items that hold meaning for you.

Symbolic Offerings and Spells: Use holly, mistletoe, and evergreen branches as offerings in seasonal rituals. Create a small charm bag with dried Yule greenery to carry with you or keep on your altar for a reminder of Yule's grounding energy throughout the holiday season.

Meditate on the Symbols' Meanings: During the solstice, take time to meditate on each symbol and its deeper meaning, letting it inspire your intentions for the year ahead. Focus on themes of resilience, rebirth, and the warmth of community to help set intentions for the winter season and beyond.

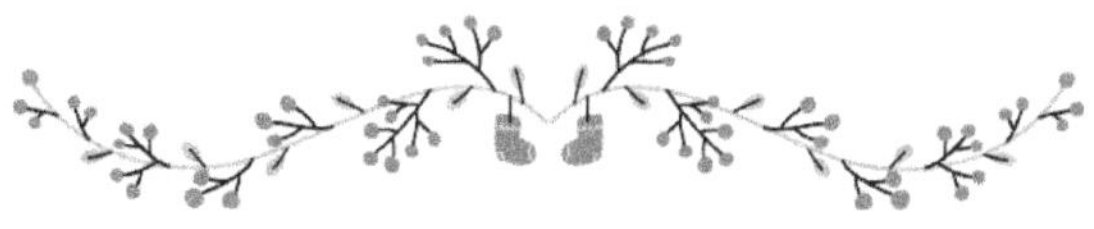

The rich symbolism of Yule, intertwined with modern holiday traditions, allows us to experience this season with more intention and spiritual depth. Each symbol carries a unique story of hope, resilience, and protection—a reminder of our connection to the natural cycles that guide and sustain us. By integrating Yule symbols into your practice, you can honour both the ancient wisdom of Yule and the enduring magic of the holiday season.

Chapter 7

RITUALS FOR SELF-CARE AND REFLECTION

The Yule season is a time for celebration, warmth, and connection, yet it can also bring with it a sense of overwhelm as we navigate gatherings, responsibilities, and the inherent busyness of the holidays. This chapter explores ways to bring the focus back to nurturing yourself through small, mindful rituals that are calm, centre, and refresh. By grounding yourself in these daily self-care practices, you can create space to reconnect with your inner peace and bring intentionality to every aspect of the season.

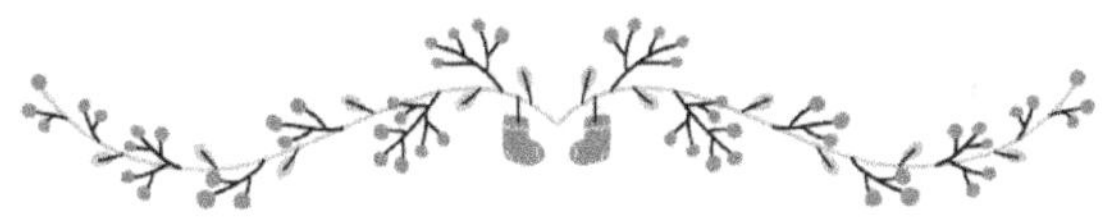

Creating a Daily Practice: Small Rituals for a Calm Holiday Season

Establishing simple, daily rituals helps you stay present and focused throughout the Yule season. These moments of mindfulness, however brief, allow you to set your intentions, express gratitude, and honour your spirit amidst the seasonal energy. A few moments in the morning and evening can set the tone for a more peaceful, joyful holiday.

Morning Affirmations: Setting Intentions for the Day

Begin each day with a positive mindset by incorporating morning affirmations into your routine. An affirmation is a powerful, present-tense statement that aligns your thoughts and energy with what you want to cultivate. For the Yule season, choose affirmations that emphasize qualities like joy, warmth, calm, and self-love.

Here are a few Yule-inspired affirmations to help you start the day with intention:

- "Today, I embrace the peace and beauty of the season."

- "I allow myself to experience joy, calm, and gratitude."

- "I am grounded, present, and open to the blessings of Yule."

- "I honour my needs and take time to nurture myself each day."

- "I am surrounded by love, warmth, and light."

Choose one affirmation each morning, saying it aloud or silently as you take a few deep breaths. You might repeat it a few times, letting the words resonate within you, or write it down to carry with you throughout the day. Let each affirmation be a gentle reminder to approach the season with a calm and open heart.

Evening Reflections: Journaling Prompts for Unwinding and Gratitude

As the day winds down, taking a few moments to reflect can provide a sense of closure and peace. Evening reflections are a chance to release any tension, express gratitude, and acknowledge the meaningful moments of the day. By journaling in the evening, you can create a grounding ritual that helps you end each day on a positive, thoughtful note.

Consider these journaling prompts to deepen your evening reflections:

- What moments of joy or beauty did I experience today?

- What am I grateful for in this season of Yule?

- Did I encounter any challenges today, and how did I navigate them?

- How did I nurture myself today? Is there anything I wish to focus on tomorrow?

- What simple joys do I look forward to tomorrow?

Take a few minutes each evening to write your responses. You don't need to fill pages; a few sentences or words can suffice. Let this practice be a gentle way to release the day's energy and set your intentions for the coming days of the Yule season.

Herbal Baths and Relaxation: A Ritual for Unwinding

One of the most soothing self-care practices is the ritual of an herbal bath. A warm bath with calming herbs allows you to release tension, clear your mind, and connect with the gentle magic of nature. During Yule, as the weather cools and we seek warmth and comfort, herbal baths can be a grounding and healing way to relax.

Choosing Herbs for a Yule Bath

Herbs carry unique energies and properties that can enhance your self-care practices. Here are a few herbs known for their relaxing, protective, and cleansing qualities—perfect for infusing a bath with calm and intention:

Lavender: Known for its soothing and calming properties, lavender encourages relaxation and is often used to ease anxiety and promote restful sleep. Lavender's soft scent can help you release tension and unwind.

Chamomile: This gentle, fragrant herb has a calming effect on the mind and body. Chamomile is particularly helpful for relieving stress, promoting relaxation, and enhancing mood.

Rosemary: Rosemary is both protective and energizing, providing a sense of warmth and clarity. It can help relieve mental fatigue and bring a sense of focus and renewal to your spirit.

Eucalyptus: With its refreshing and purifying aroma, eucalyptus is known to clear the mind and create a sense of calm. It can also be helpful for alleviating seasonal congestion.

Juniper Berries: Juniper is protective and cleansing, and it has long been used to dispel negative energy. Adding juniper berries to your bath can help you feel renewed and grounded.

Creating Your Herbal Bath

Follow these steps to create your own herbal bath, using the ingredients and intentions that resonate most with you.

- Gather your herbs: Choose two to three herbs that you feel drawn to. You can use dried or fresh herbs, or add a few drops of essential oils to enhance the fragrance and benefits. If you're using essential oils, start with just a few drops, as they can be potent.

- Prepare an herbal sachet: To prevent loose herbs from clogging your drain, place them in a cloth sachet or muslin bag. You can also use a tea infuser if you prefer a smaller, concentrated infusion.

- Set your intention: As you prepare your bath, take a moment to set an intention. Perhaps you wish to release stress, clear your mind, or simply enjoy a quiet moment of peace. Hold this intention in your mind as you add the herbs to the bath.

- Draw the bath: Run warm water and add your herbal sachet or essential oils. Let the water fill the room with the calming scents and give yourself a moment to enjoy the aroma.

- Soak and relax: Step into the bath and let yourself relax. You might visualize any tension or worry melting away, carried by the water. Take deep breaths, focusing on the calming scents and sensations. You may even wish to add a few crystals, such as amethyst for relaxation or rose quartz for self-love, to enhance the energy of the bath.

- Reflect and release: As you finish your bath, imagine any lingering stress or negativity being absorbed by the water. Allow yourself to feel renewed and grounded, ready to embrace the warmth and joy of the Yule season.

Connecting to Nature and Seasonal Traditions

Infusing your self-care rituals with seasonal elements can bring a sense of spiritual fulfilment and a connection to the world around you. Whether it's stepping outside for a mindful walk, using pine or cedar as seasonal scents, or decorating with natural Yule symbols, finding ways to incorporate nature deepens your connection to the cycle of the year. Observing natural cycles—such as the winter solstice, the lengthening of days, or even the bare branches of winter—can add personal meaning and spiritual enrichment to your practices.

Embracing Self-Care as a Seasonal Ritual

Self-care during the holiday season is about finding small, meaningful ways to honour your well-being and keep your spirit nourished. These daily practices—morning affirmations, evening reflections, and herbal baths—are gentle reminders that you deserve rest, joy, and peace. By embracing these rituals, you're not only caring for yourself; you're also deepening your connection to the quiet magic of Yule, creating a season filled with mindfulness, warmth, and grace.

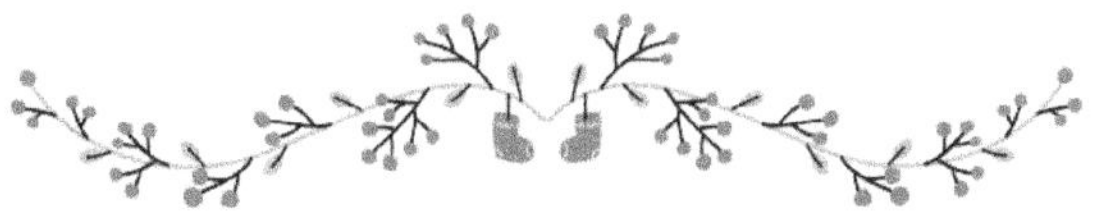

The holidays can be a time of transformation and renewal, and these self-care rituals offer simple yet profound ways to keep yourself centred amidst it all. As you honour your needs, you create the inner harmony to enjoy the blessings of the season.

Chapter 8

NOURISHMENT AND SEASONAL FOODS

As winter deepens and Yule approaches, the magic of the season finds its way into our kitchens, bringing warmth and nourishment to our tables. In many traditions, food has always held a central place in celebrations, symbolizing abundance, comfort, and togetherness. In this chapter, we'll explore recipes that evoke the spirit of Yule—cozy, nourishing dishes and drinks infused with the flavours of the season. Alongside these magical recipes, we'll share ways to cultivate a mindful approach to eating, allowing you to savour the richness of holiday meals with presence and gratitude.

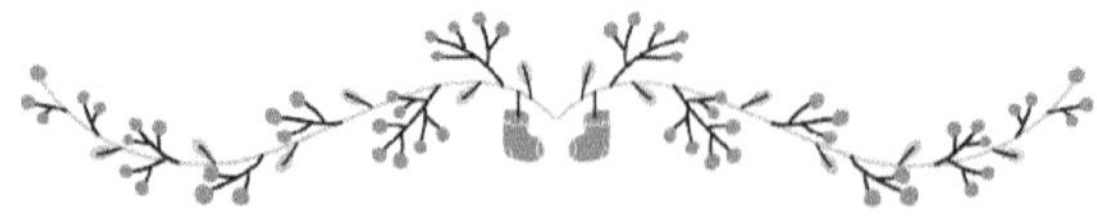

Seasonal Nourishment: A Return to Comforting, Intentional Foods

Winter invites us to slow down and turn inward, and the foods of the season mirror this shift. Warming, hearty ingredients, like root vegetables, spices, and rich broths, provide comfort and sustenance. Embrace the magic of the kitchen by preparing nourishing recipes that honour Yule's themes of light, warmth, and abundance. When you infuse your cooking with intention, each meal becomes a celebration of the season's gifts.

The Power of Food for Mental Well-being

The holiday season can bring heightened stress, with increased demands on time, energy, and mental health. Certain ingredients, known for their calming and mood-boosting properties, can provide gentle support during these times. Incorporate ingredients like dark leafy greens, which are high in magnesium and promote relaxation, or foods rich in omega-3 fatty acids—such as walnuts or flaxseed—which help stabilize mood. Foods rich in tryptophan, like oats, nuts, and seeds, support serotonin production, enhancing a sense of calm. By choosing foods that support mental well-being, you nurture both body and spirit during this potentially challenging season.

Magical Recipes: Warming Dishes and Drinks for the Season

These recipes are designed to bring warmth and comfort, evoking the essence of Yule's energy. As you cook, keep in mind the magical qualities of the ingredients and the intentions they bring into your space.

Spiced Yule Cider: Warm, spiced cider is a quintessential winter drink, perfect for gatherings or quiet moments by the fire. Apples are symbols of love and healing, while warming spices like cinnamon and cloves bring protection and vitality to the holiday season.

Ingredients:

- 6 cups apple cider or juice

- 1 orange, thinly sliced

- 3 cinnamon sticks

- 4 whole cloves

- 2-3 star anise pods

- 1 inch fresh ginger, sliced

- Optional: a splash of cranberry juice for colour and tartness

Instructions:

1. In a large pot, combine the apple cider, orange slices, cinnamon sticks, cloves, star anise, and ginger.

2. Bring the mixture to a gentle simmer over medium heat, then reduce to low and let it warm for 20-30 minutes to allow the flavours to blend.

3. Strain if desired, then ladle into mugs. Garnish with a cinnamon stick or orange slice for a festive touch.

Magical Intentions: As you stir the cider, think of the warmth you want to bring into your home and heart this season. Visualize your intentions for peace, health, and happiness being infused into each cup.

Winter Root Vegetable Soup: A hearty, nourishing soup made with root vegetables, this recipe embodies the grounding energy of winter. Root vegetables like carrots, potatoes, and parsnips offer stability and warmth, while herbs such as thyme and rosemary provide protection and resilience.

Ingredients:

- 2 tablespoons olive oil

- 1 large onion, diced

- 2 garlic cloves, minced

- 2 carrots, sliced

- 2 parsnips, sliced

- 2 medium potatoes, cubed

- 1 sweet potato or yam, cubed

- 6 cups vegetable broth

- 1-2 sprigs of fresh thyme

- 1 sprig of rosemary

- Salt and pepper to taste

- Optional: a handful of kale or spinach for added nutrients

Instructions:

1. Heat the olive oil in a large pot over medium heat. Add the onion and garlic, sautéing until softened.

2. Add the carrots, parsnips, potatoes, and sweet potato, stirring to coat them in the oil.

3. Pour in the vegetable broth and add the thyme and rosemary. Bring the mixture to a boil, then reduce the heat and let it simmer for 20-30 minutes, or until the vegetables are tender.

4. Season with salt and pepper to taste. For extra greens, stir in kale or spinach at the end, letting it wilt before serving.

Magical Intentions: Visualize the grounding energy of the earth nourishing you through this meal, bringing strength and resilience for the season ahead.

Yule Hearth Bread Baking bread is a ritual in itself, and Yule Hearth Bread is no exception. This simple yet delicious bread, made with honey and warm spices, fills your home with a comforting aroma. Honey brings sweetness and warmth, while spices like cinnamon and nutmeg add a protective, festive energy.

Ingredients:

- 2 ¼ teaspoons active dry yeast

- 1 ½ cups warm water

- 2 tablespoons honey

- 3 ½ cups all-purpose or whole wheat flour

- 1 teaspoon salt

- 1 teaspoon cinnamon

- ½ teaspoon nutmeg

Instructions:

1. In a small bowl, dissolve the yeast in warm water with the honey. Let sit for 5-10 minutes until foamy.

2. In a large mixing bowl, combine the flour, salt, cinnamon, and nutmeg. Pour in the yeast mixture and stir until a dough forms.

3. Knead the dough on a lightly floured surface for about 10 minutes, until smooth and elastic.

4. Place the dough in a greased bowl, cover, and let it rise in a warm place for about an hour, or until doubled in size.

5. Punch down the dough and shape it into a loaf. Place it on a baking sheet or in a loaf pan, cover, and let it rise for another 30 minutes.

6. Preheat the oven to 375°F (190°C). Bake for 25-30 minutes, or until golden brown. Let cool slightly before slicing.

Magical Intentions: As you knead the dough, imagine infusing it with warmth, abundance, and love. Visualize the bread as a source of comfort and grounding for yourself and those who share in it.

Mindful Eating Practices: Savouring Holiday Foods with Gratitude

During the holiday season, we often rush through meals or overindulging with little awareness. By adopting a mindful approach to eating, you can enhance your connection to food and the joy it brings. Mindful eating is about savouring each bite, appreciating the flavours, and honouring the time and care that went into preparing the meal.

Tips for Mindful Eating

Set an Intention Before You Eat: Before starting a meal, take a moment to pause, breathe, and set an intention. This could be as simple as giving thanks for the food or visualizing nourishment and warmth entering your body.

Engage All Your Senses: Notice the colours, textures, and aromas of your meal. Take a moment to appreciate the visual appeal, the scent, and even the sounds as you prepare or serve it.

Savour Each Bite: Take your time, focusing on the flavours and textures with each mouthful. Chew slowly and allow yourself to fully experience each taste, noticing how it changes and develops.

Practice Gratitude: Reflect on the sources of your food—the farmers, the ingredients, and the preparation process. By acknowledging the journey that brought each ingredient to your table, you connect to the abundance of nature and the spirit of Yule.

Honour Your Body's Needs: Listen to your body's hunger and fullness cues. Eat what makes you feel good, and stop when you feel satisfied, honouring your body's wisdom.

Setting Boundaries During Holiday Gatherings

Holiday gatherings can bring a mix of joy and emotional fatigue, especially if you're navigating family dynamics or a packed schedule. Give yourself permission to set boundaries around holiday meals and gatherings. Prioritize self-care, and remember that it's okay to say no to additional helpings or skip a dish if it doesn't resonate with you. You deserve to feel nourished, not overwhelmed.

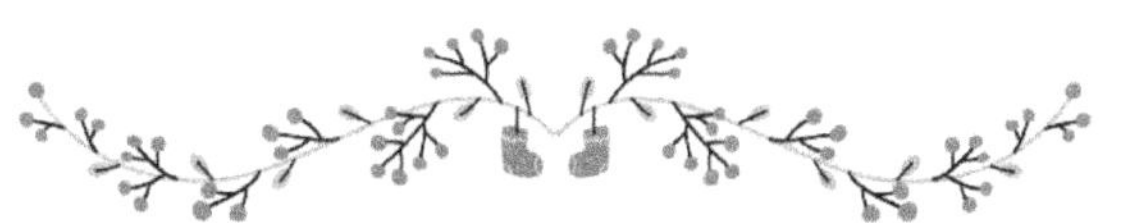

Nourishing yourself during Yule goes beyond the ingredients or recipes—it's about bringing awareness, gratitude, and a sense of ritual into the kitchen. Each meal and drink becomes a celebration of the season's magic, warming not just your body but also your spirit. Through these recipes and mindful eating practices, you can create a holiday experience that feels both delicious and fulfilling, grounding you in the present moment as you enjoy the gifts of Yule.

Chapter 9

HOLIDAY CRAFTING AND DECORATION

Bringing the spirit of Yule into your home can be a beautiful, grounding experience. This season's traditional crafts and decorations connect us to the natural world, encouraging us to work with elements that honour winter's beauty and magic. With every Yule log, wreath, and charm bottle, we weave our intentions and energy into the season, creating a warm, welcoming space filled with meaning.

In this chapter, you'll find step-by-step instructions for crafting Yule-inspired decorations and handmade gifts that radiate the magic of the season, from intentional ornaments to blessing jars filled with love, protection, and prosperity.

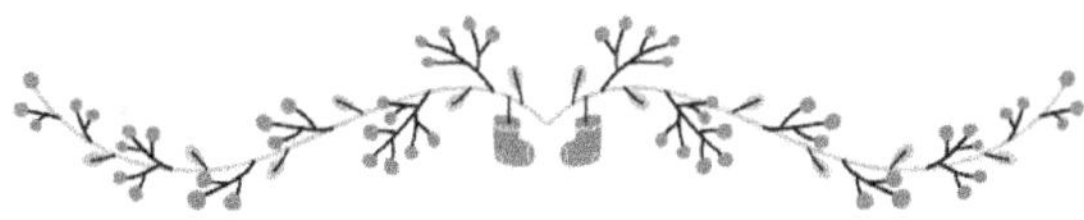

Crafting and Mindfulness: Embracing Calm and Clarity During the Holidays

The holiday season can be an emotionally challenging time, as we face added social obligations and expectations. Crafting can be a therapeutic practice, helping to manage feelings of anxiety, loneliness, or seasonal blues. Creating something with your hands offers a mindful break, a chance to focus on the present moment, and a way to channel emotions constructively. As you engage in each craft in this chapter, let yourself sink into the rhythm of the activity—your hands grounding you, your focus centreing you. By embracing these moments of creative focus, you can use holiday crafting as a gentle way to nourish your mental health and bring a sense of peace into the season.

Yule Crafts and Decor: Infusing Your Space with Seasonal Magic

Crafting a Yule Log

The Yule log is one of the season's most ancient symbols, representing warmth, light, and the promise of brighter days ahead. Traditionally, a Yule log is burned to welcome the return of the sun after the winter solstice. Today, a decorative Yule log can symbolize these same energies, even if you don't have a fireplace to burn it in.

Materials Needed:

- A small, sturdy log (birch, oak, or pine are ideal for their magical properties)

- Three small candles (red for vitality, green for growth, white for purity)

- Twine or natural ribbon

- Evergreen branches, pinecones, and other natural decorations

- Dried herbs (such as rosemary for protection, sage for cleansing, and cinnamon sticks for prosperity)

Instructions:

1. Select Your Log: Choose a log that resonates with you, one that feels sturdy and warm. If possible, use a piece of wood with personal meaning

or gather it during a nature walk with gratitude.

2. Decorate the Log: Arrange evergreen branches, pinecones, cinnamon sticks, and other natural elements around the log, securing them with twine or natural ribbon.

3. Attach the Candles: Secure the candles on top of the log, spaced evenly. Be mindful that they will not tip over if you plan to burn them.

4. Set Your Intentions: As you arrange each item on the log, think about the intentions you want to set for the coming year. Light each candle with a specific wish—prosperity, love, health, or whatever aligns with your personal goals for the year.

5. Using the Yule Log: If you're able to safely burn your Yule log, do so with intention, visualizing your wishes taking root and growing. If it's decorative, keep it in a place of honour in your home, where you can reflect on your intentions throughout the season.

Natural Wreaths

Wreaths made from evergreens, holly, or pine embody the spirit of Yule and bring the outdoors into your home, adding both beauty and protection to your space. Incorporating elements like berries, dried flowers, or even found objects from nature, such as acorns or branches, can further align your wreath with the current season and your environment.

Materials Needed:

- A grapevine or metal wreath frame

- Fresh or dried evergreen branches (pine, cedar, or holly)

- Pinecones, berries, cinnamon sticks, or dried citrus slices

- Floral wire or twine

Instructions:

1. Prepare the Frame: Secure branches to your wreath frame using floral wire or twine, layering each branch until the frame is covered.

2. Add Seasonal Accents: Decorate with pinecones, berries, dried citrus, or cinnamon sticks for extra charm.

3. Set Your Intentions: As you work, focus on the protective and abundant qualities of each element. Visualize the wreath as a shield for your home, filled with warmth and peace.

4. Hanging Your Wreath: Place your wreath on your front door or in a central room. Whenever you see it, remember the intentions you've woven into its branches.

Intentional Ornaments: Magic for the New Year

Ornaments can become vessels for intentions, carrying blessings for the new year. Handmade ornaments hold powerful, personalized energy, making them wonderful additions to your Yule decorations.

DIY Intention Ornaments Materials Needed:

Materials Needed:

- Clear, fillable ornaments (glass or plastic)

- Small crystals, dried herbs, or written intentions

- Ribbon or twine for hanging

Instructions:

1. Select Items with Meaning: Choose small items to fill the ornament based on your intentions. For example:

2. Dried lavender for peace

3. Rosemary for protection

4. Small crystals like amethyst for clarity or rose quartz for love

5. Fill the Ornament: Carefully add these items into the ornament. You can also write a short affirmation or wish on a small piece of paper and place it inside.

6. Hang with Intention: Hang the ornament where it will remind you of the intentions it holds, such as on your tree, near a window, or in a central area.

Balancing the Joy of Giving and Receiving: Thoughtful Creations for Loved Ones

Handmade gifts offer a unique way to balance the spirit of giving and receiving. When you create a gift with intention, it becomes a vessel for positive energy that will uplift the recipient long after the season ends. Handmade gifts not only symbolize warmth and love but also provide a break from the commercial aspects of the holidays. By focusing on these meaningful exchanges, you foster connections based on thoughtfulness and appreciation, rather than material expectations.

Infused Herbal Sachets

Herbal sachets are simple but powerful gifts that carry the magic of plants. These small bundles can be tucked into drawers, under pillows, or even in a car for a constant source of calming energy.

Materials Needed:

- Small cloth bags or squares of fabric

- Dried herbs (like lavender for relaxation, chamomile for peace, rosemary for protection)

- A ribbon or string to tie the sachet

Instructions:

1. Choose Herbs for the Recipient's Needs: Think about what the re-

cipient might benefit from. For example, lavender and chamomile are perfect for someone seeking calm, while rosemary and bay leaves are protective.

2. Assemble the Sachet: Place the herbs in the cloth bag, focusing on your intention as you work. Tie the sachet closed with ribbon.

3. Bless the Sachet: Hold it in your hands and set an intention for the recipient, visualizing your wish for them filling the sachet.

Intention Candles

Creating intention candles is a beautiful way to craft a unique, personal gift for loved ones. By adding specific herbs, oils, and colours, each candle becomes a tool for focus and manifestation.

Materials Needed:

- Soy or beeswax candle (or a clear candle container and wax flakes)

- Essential oils (such as lavender for peace, orange for joy, cinnamon for abundance)

- Herbs or dried flowers for decoration

- A wick, if you're making your own candle from scratch

Instructions:

1. Melt the Wax (if making your own candle): Melt the wax slowly and add a few drops of essential oils.

2. Add Herbs with Intention: Sprinkle herbs or dried flowers into the candle, setting an intention with each one.

3. Allow to Set: Let the candle solidify fully before decorating or gifting. You may wish to write a small note explaining its intended energy to the recipient.

Blessing Jars and Charm Bottles

Blessing jars and charm bottles are tiny, magical tokens filled with symbols of love, protection, and prosperity. These are perfect gifts for friends or family members who appreciate a little extra magic.

Materials Needed:

- Small glass jars or bottles with corks or lids

- Small items such as crystals, herbs, charms, and written affirmations

- Ribbon, string, or wax for sealing

Instructions:

1. Fill the Jar with Intentions: Add small items that represent different blessings. For example: Amethyst for clarity, Cloves for protection, Dried orange peel for joy

2. Seal with Intention: Once filled, seal the jar with ribbon or wax. Hold it in your hands, visualizing the blessings you wish to bestow upon the recipient.

3. Present with a Heartfelt Message: Include a note explaining the charm's meaning, encouraging the recipient to keep it in a special place as a reminder of your well-wishes.

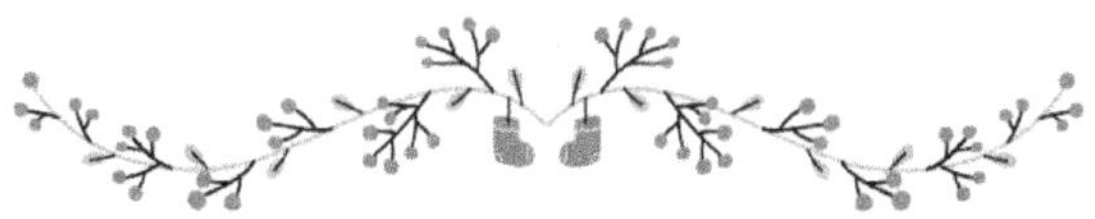

By mindfully crafting during the holiday season, you're not only creating decorations and gifts but also nurturing your well-being, connecting to nature, and honouring the spirit of giving and receiving. Each piece carries your energy and intentions, and with these mindful practices, the spirit of Yule will bring warmth, peace, and joy into your home and the lives of those you love.

Chapter 10

NATURE WALKS AND REFLECTIONS

Winter's quieter energy offers a unique opportunity to connect with the rhythms of nature, even in the colder months. Though the world may seem dormant, a walk in the winter landscape reveals subtle signs of life, resilience, and beauty. Spending time outdoors during Yule season, even briefly, grounds us and reminds us of the cycles of rest, renewal, and growth. The holiday season can be emotionally intense, but nature offers a gentle balm, helping to reduce anxiety, lift our moods, and support mental clarity.

This chapter offers ways to incorporate winter nature walks into your holiday season, with reflection exercises and journaling prompts that allow you to draw meaning and inspiration from the surrounding landscape.

Connecting with Winter Nature: Embracing the Beauty of the Season

Even when snow blankets the ground and the trees stand bare, the winter landscape is alive with gentle beauty. Embracing winter's natural stillness helps us find peace in a season that can often be overwhelming. Just as nature retreats to gather strength for the coming spring, we, too, can take this time to slow down, reflect, and recharge. Winter walks encourage us to notice the quiet transformations of the natural world, like frost glistening on leaves, the tracks of animals in the snow, or the warm glow of winter sunlight. Studies show that spending time in nature can improve our mental health by reducing anxiety, alleviating stress, and enhancing our mood, which is particularly beneficial during the holidays.

Nature Walk Exercises

Breathing with the Season

Focus: Grounding and calming

Exercise: As you begin your walk, pause and take three deep breaths, inhaling the crisp winter air and exhaling any tension or stress. With each breath, imagine connecting more deeply with the earth beneath you, feeling rooted and steady. If possible, take a moment to listen to the surrounding silence, allowing the quiet of winter to bring peace to your mind.

Observing the Landscape

Focus: Mindfulness and awareness

Exercise: As you walk, observe the unique beauty of winter around you. Notice how trees, stripped of leaves, reveal their intricate branches. Look for traces of life—animal tracks in the snow, birds in the trees, or frost patterns on stones. Try to find three small details in the landscape that resonate with you, appreciating their subtlety and connection to the season.

Gathering Natural Elements

Focus: Finding magic in the small details

Exercise: Look for small items to collect on your walk, like pinecones, stones, dried leaves, or berries. These simple treasures can be used in your holiday decor or for personal reflection. When you gather each item, thank nature for offering it to you, bringing a spirit of gratitude and respect to your walk.

Maintaining Balance: Sharing Nature Walks and Setting Boundaries

The holidays can often bring emotional fatigue and burnout from social expectations, making it easy to lose ourselves in giving and neglect the importance of receiving support. Taking time for a nature walk, whether alone or shared with loved ones, is a powerful way to recharge and balance these dynamics. If you choose to invite others on your walk, share the experience of noticing winter's beauty and allow the balance of giving and receiving to flow naturally through your shared observations.

Remember, setting boundaries to make time for self-care is essential. Prioritize your nature walks as a non-negotiable part of your routine, even if only for a short time each day. Protecting these moments helps you return to social gatherings with a renewed sense of energy and calm.

Seasonal Reflection Prompts: Journaling with Nature's Wisdom

Winter's slower pace invites us to reflect and recharge, just as nature prepares for a new cycle of growth. Taking time to journal after a nature walk allows us to explore themes of rest, renewal, and release, helping us align with winter's natural energy. These prompts can be completed after a walk or whenever you feel drawn to reconnect with the season's quieter spirit.

Prompt 1: Winter's Gift of Stillness

- As you reflect on your walk, think about what you noticed in the land-scape. How did winter's stillness make you feel?

- Write about what you can release or put on hold for now, just as nature slows down to conserve energy.

- How can you welcome moments of stillness into your life, even after the holiday season?

Prompt 2: Finding Light in the Darkness

- Winter solstice, the longest night of the year, symbolizes the turning point toward brighter days. What sources of light—both literal and metaphorical—bring warmth and hope to your life during winter?

- Consider what "light" you can share with others. Is there a way you can embody kindness, love, or hope in the coming year?

Prompt 3: Embracing the Season of Renewal

- Think of something you've been carrying with you throughout the past year. What would you like to let go of or transform as the year turns?

- Consider setting a small intention that honours the season of rest and renewal. How can you create space in your life for rest, growth, and healing?

Prompt 4: Lessons from Winter's Resilience

- The trees and plants around us endure winter's cold, surviving without their usual vibrancy, yet they stand strong and await spring. In what ways do you see resilience in nature?

- Write about how you can nurture your own resilience. What inner strengths can you honour as you prepare for the new year?

Integrating Yule Traditions into Nature Walks

For those who celebrate Yule, the season holds special significance, honouring themes of rebirth, light, and connection to nature. To connect more deeply with seasonal traditions, consider gathering specific items such as evergreen sprigs, pinecones, or holly to create a Yule altar at home, symbolizing winter's promise of renewed life. During your walk, you might even perform a small ritual by whispering intentions or blessings as you touch the bark of a tree or place a stone by a stream, allowing your gratitude and hopes to become part of the natural landscape.

Bringing Nature Home: Using Gathered Materials for Reflection

After your walk, place the items you gathered in a small dish or on a dedicated altar space. These objects can serve as gentle reminders of winter's wisdom. Each time you see them, let them guide you back to the peace and calm you felt outdoors. Here are a few ways to incorporate them into your seasonal practice:

Pinecones and Stones for Meditation: Use these as touchstones during meditation. Hold them in your hands, feeling their texture and weight, allowing yourself to stay grounded as you reflect.

Creating a Winter Altar: Place gathered items on a small altar space. Add a candle, and, if possible, some evergreen sprigs or dried flowers. This space can become a seasonal sanctuary for introspection, where you can write, meditate, or simply sit quietly.

Seasonal Nature Journal: Attach a small pinecone, leaf, or photo from your walk to a journal page. Reflect on what you observed during your walk, jotting down any thoughts, feelings, or lessons that came up for you. Over time, this journal can serve as a record of your connection with the natural cycles.

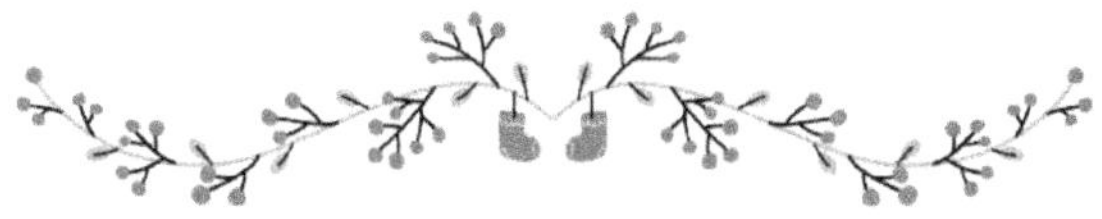

Though winter may seem like a time of stillness, it's a season of quiet magic, where nature teaches us the value of patience, resilience, and introspection. Through mindful nature walks and reflective practices, you can connect with winter's subtle gifts, finding meaning and comfort in its slower pace. By spending time outdoors and embracing the season's lessons, we become more attuned to the cycles of rest and renewal that are part of all life. Let winter's muted power nurture your spirit, reminding you to honour your own rhythms and rest, knowing that brighter days will come.

Chapter 11

BUILDING COMMUNITY AND CONNECTION

The holiday season is a natural time to draw closer to the people we cherish. As the world quiets in winter, gathering with friends, family, and neighbours can bring warmth and connection, reminding us of the joy found in shared traditions, kindness, and companionship. Whether hosting a simple gathering or extending a hand to your community, embracing the season's spirit of connection enriches the holidays and uplifts everyone involved.

In this chapter, we explore ways to celebrate the Yule season with loved ones through mindful gatherings, exchanges, and acts of kindness. By building community with intention, we honour the magic of human connection and the spirit of giving.

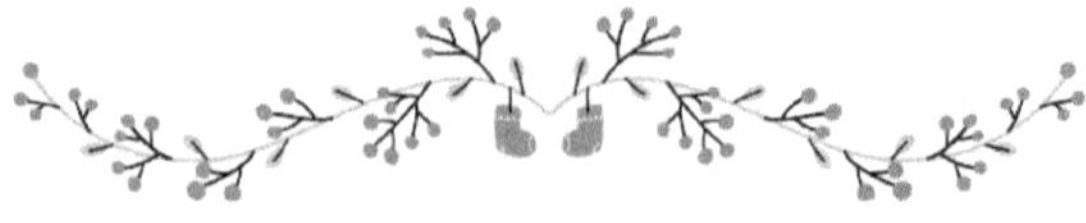

Managing Holiday Stress and Overwhelm

The holiday season can be both joyful and overwhelming, especially in hosting gatherings or taking part in community events. Planning and organizing can add stress, so it's essential to stay grounded and avoid burnout. Here are some tips for managing holiday stress and keeping things manageable:

Set Realistic Expectations: Limit yourself to what's feasible without straining your energy or resources. It's okay to simplify gatherings, delegate tasks, or even skip certain traditions if they feel burdensome.

Plan Ahead and Delegate: Create a schedule, and consider asking friends or family to contribute. Whether it's bringing food, helping with setup, or providing entertainment, sharing responsibilities helps keep gatherings enjoyable.

Take Time for Yourself: Scheduling moments of quiet and rest allows you to recharge, especially during the busier times. Remember, it's okay to step away for a few minutes to breathe, meditate, or simply reflect.

Supporting Mental Health During the Holidays

The holidays can be particularly challenging for those who struggle with mental health. Feelings of loneliness, stress, or sadness can arise, even amid gatherings. Building community and connection can be a powerful way to support mental well-being. Foster a network of supportive relationships and remind yourself and others of the importance of reaching out:

Stay Connected: Seek opportunities to engage with friends, family, or community events that feel comfortable and supportive. Even a brief conversation or shared meal can lift the spirits.

Offer and Accept Support: Be mindful of others who may feel isolated or stressed, and offer kindness where possible. Likewise, if you're struggling, consider reaching out to someone who understands. Letting people in can make a profound difference.

Yule Gatherings and Celebrations: Bringing Meaning into Your Time Together

Gathering with friends and family can be one of the most fulfilling parts of the holiday season. From intimate, candle-lit evenings to cozy potluck dinners, there are many ways to come together with intention, sharing warmth and light in the spirit of Yule.

Potluck Dinners and Candle-Lit Gatherings

Hosting a holiday potluck or candle-lit gathering brings people together in a way that feels personal, meaningful, and relaxed. Here are a few ideas to keep these gatherings simple yet magical:

Potluck Dinner with Intention: Ask each guest to bring a dish that has a special meaning to them, perhaps a family recipe or a food that brings them comfort. Before you eat, invite everyone to share a short story about their dish or what they are grateful for this season. This turns the meal into a tapestry of shared memories and blessings.

Candle-Lit Reflection Evening: Invite friends over for an evening of quiet reflection. Set up candles around the room and ask each guest to bring one to light in honour of a wish, blessing, or intention for the coming year. Let the soft glow of the candles create an intimate atmosphere for sharing and contemplation.

Storytelling Circle: Create a circle where each person shares a memory or story from their year. Encourage themes of gratitude, resilience, or laughter. Storytelling not only connects us but allows us to honour each other's experiences, deepening the bonds within the group.

Hosting a Yule Exchange

The tradition of gift-giving can be a beautiful way to celebrate the connections we have, especially when gifts are chosen with intention and thought. Hosting a "Yule Exchange" invites your community to exchange small, meaningful gifts as symbols of love and connection, bringing warmth and joy to the winter season.

How to Host a Yule Exchange:

Set the Tone: When inviting your friends or family, encourage them to bring a gift that carries meaning, whether handmade, found in nature, or symbolic of a shared memory. The focus should be on the thought and intention behind the gift, rather than on material value.

Circle of Giving: Gather in a circle and take turns giving your gift, sharing a few words about why you chose it or what you hope it will bring to the recipient. This ritualizes the act of giving, making it about connection rather than exchange.

Ideas for Simple Intentional Gifts:

- Small charm bottles with protective herbs and symbols

- A handwritten letter of gratitude or a poem

- A crystal or stone that represents qualities the giver admires in the recipient

- Handmade candles, soap, or infused oils for seasonal warmth

Incorporating Nature and Seasonal Elements

Connecting with nature and the changing seasons brings a grounding energy to holiday gatherings. Consider adding natural elements to your decorations and gatherings to reflect the beauty of the winter season.

Use Seasonal Greenery: Decorate with pine, holly, or eucalyptus for a natural touch, or create a wreath from branches collected on a nature walk. These elements honour the season and bring a refreshing aroma to your space.

Outdoor Celebrations: Weather permitting, consider hosting part of your gathering outdoors. A bonfire, winter picnic, or stargazing night can create a memorable connection to nature, and the crisp air provides a refreshing change of pace.

Setting Boundaries and Managing Social Obligations

While social events can bring joy, they can also lead to emotional fatigue and burnout. Managing social obligations thoughtfully allows you to participate while also taking care of your well-being:

Say "No" When Needed: It's okay to set limits. Politely decline events or set boundaries around time commitments when you're feeling overwhelmed. Prioritizing a few meaningful gatherings can be more fulfilling than attending every event.

Create Balance: Find a balance between social and private time. Taking breaks between events and planning time for yourself helps prevent burnout and allows you to fully enjoy the gatherings you do attend.

Acts of Kindness: Embodying the Giving Spirit of the Season

The essence of the Yule season is found in acts of kindness and generosity. Taking time to give back, both within your circle and in your larger community, reflects the magic of the season, spreading warmth and joy beyond our immediate world. Here are a few ways to embrace the giving spirit:

Practices for Community: Small Acts with Big Impact

Community Volunteering

Consider volunteering at a local shelter, food bank, or community centre. Giving your time and energy in support of others is one of the most meaningful ways to embody the season's spirit. Bringing friends along can turn it into a shared experience of compassion and goodwill.

Organizing a Neighbourhood Yule Fest

A small neighbourhood gathering, like a Yule fest, brings people together and fosters community spirit. Arrange for an outdoor gathering where neighbours can enjoy hot cider, seasonal treats, and music. If possible, include an activity for children or offer a small "Yule blessing" ceremony for those who wish to participate.

Acts of Kindness in Everyday Life

Kindness doesn't need to be grand to have an impact. Consider spreading warmth with small acts: bake extra cookies for a neighbour, send a handwritten note to someone who's been on your mind, or help a friend with holiday errands. These simple gestures remind us that we're all connected.

Creating a Blessing Jar for Your Community

Set out a "Blessing Jar" in a community space, such as your workplace, neighbourhood coffee shop, or local community centre. Invite people to write a short blessing, positive thought, or intention and place it in the jar. On the winter solstice or during a Yule celebration, share some of these blessings aloud as a collective reminder of gratitude and kindness.

Whether in the company of loved ones or through acts of service, the holidays present countless opportunities to spread warmth, build community, and connect with others. Celebrating Yule is about creating and sharing a meaningful experience, reminding us that the most valuable gifts come from the heart.

Embrace this season of giving as a time to nourish and inspire each other, cultivating kindness and goodwill that lasts well beyond winter's close. In building a community rooted in love, gratitude, and mutual support, we embody the true magic of Yule and the enduring beauty of the holiday spirit.

Chapter 12

MINDFUL MAGIC PRACTICES FOR THE SEASON

The Yule season invites reflection, offering an opportunity to connect deeply with traditions, nature, and community. Through mindful practices like meditation, journaling, and affirmations, we can cultivate a sense of inner peace and connection with the season's magic. This chapter explores ways to balance the beauty of giving and receiving, reconnect with seasonal traditions, and prioritize well-being amidst the holiday's social demands.

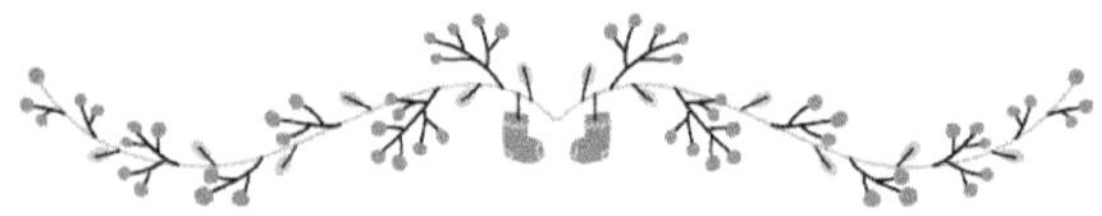

Meditations and Affirmations for Seasonal Renewal

Embracing Light Meditation

As Yule celebrates the return of light after the winter solstice, this gentle meditation helps you connect with themes of renewal and warmth. Practicing it at sunrise or during a quiet moment can offer grounding during holiday stress.

Guided Meditation

1. Find a comfortable, quiet space to sit or lie down.

2. Close your eyes, taking deep breaths and relaxing with each exhale.

3. Visualize a gentle light rising within, filling you with warmth and calm.

4. Let the light expand, surrounding you in a peaceful glow.

5. Reflect on what the return of light means to you—be it hope, clarity, or peace.

6. After a few minutes, slowly rejoin your surroundings, carrying this warmth with you.

Affirmations for Renewal and Hope

Affirmations invite positive intentions, aligning our mindsets with what we wish to foster. Inspired by Yule's themes, these affirmations can be a grounding way to greet each day:

- "I welcome the light of renewal and embrace the opportunities it brings."

- "As the days grow brighter, I open my heart to hope and possibility."

- "I am grounded, calm, and connected to the spirit of the season."

Reconnecting with Seasonal Traditions

In today's fast-paced world, reconnecting with natural, seasonal elements helps foster a sense of rootedness. Traditional Yule practices like using evergreens, seasonal herbs, or meditative rituals can strengthen our connection to nature and heritage. Consider bringing these elements into your celebrations:

Using Seasonal Greenery: Decorate with evergreens, pinecones, and holly, symbolizing life and endurance. These natural touches create a calming atmosphere that celebrates the season's beauty.

Outdoor Meditations: Bundle up and meditate in nature, even if just for a few moments. Breathing in the crisp winter air can offer clarity and a sense of connection to the natural world.

Incorporating Herbs in Rituals: Lavender, cedar, and rosemary can enhance rituals and meditations with their grounding scents, helping you feel connected to both earth and tradition.

Creating a Yule Grimoire

Keeping a record of the season's rituals, reflections, and intentions is a powerful way to deepen one's connection with Yule. A Yule Grimoire—or holiday journal—serves as a personal archive, capturing the unique experiences and insights that emerge each year.

Documenting Rituals and Recipes

A Grimoire is a wonderful place to document seasonal traditions, whether they're recipes, spells, or personal reflections. Encourage readers to see this as a living document that grows and changes with each holiday season, reflecting both their personal journey and the magic of Yule.

Suggested Grimoire Entries:

Recipes: Record any special holiday recipes, from spiced cider to herbal blends for self-care. Note any magical intentions or ingredients used, along with reflections on the meaning or memories associated with the dish.

Affirmations and Intentions: Write seasonal affirmations and any intentions set for the season. Over the years, these entries can become a source of insight and growth, showing how one's priorities and intentions evolve.

Ritual Reflections: After engaging in a ritual, take a few moments to record thoughts, emotions, and any significant experiences. This might include reflections on the Embracing Light meditation, personal insights, or messages received during moments of stillness.

Creating Templates for Consistency:

To make Grimoire entries a seamless and consistent practice, offer readers a few simple templates:

Ritual Entry Template

Name of Ritual:

Date & Time:

Purpose of the Ritual:

Materials Used:

Description of the Experience:

Reflections and Insights:

Recipe Entry Template

Name of Recipe:

Ingredients:

Preparation Steps:

Magical Intentions:

Family or Personal Meaning:

Notes for Next Time:

By taking time to write, reflect, and engage with the season in a meaningful way, readers will find that their Grimoire becomes a treasured source of wisdom, grounding, and inspiration. This chapter invites readers to welcome the Yule season with practices that bring calm, connection, and mindful magic into their everyday lives.

Finding Balance Between Giving and Receiving

The holidays can easily become focused on giving, leaving us feeling emotionally drained. Building balance is essential to feel fulfilled and refreshed, rather than overwhelmed. Sharing these mindfulness practices with loved ones, like joining in affirmations or meditations together, can foster this balance. Simple traditions of reciprocal kindness can turn gatherings into opportunities for mutual exchange, enriching both the giver and receiver.

Setting Boundaries for Self-Care

Amid holiday social expectations, it's easy to feel emotionally fatigued. Making time for yourself is crucial, even when the season's demands pull you in different directions. Setting boundaries helps you avoid burnout and maintain a sense of calm:

Limit Social Obligations: It's okay to prioritize events or gatherings that genuinely uplift you. Give yourself permission to decline invitations when you need a quiet evening.

Create Time for Mindfulness: Even amidst the festivities, set aside a few minutes for personal mindfulness practices, such as journaling, meditating, or practicing affirmations.

Communicate Your Needs: Let loved ones know if you need space or time for self-care, emphasizing that this allows you to fully enjoy and engage with the holiday season.

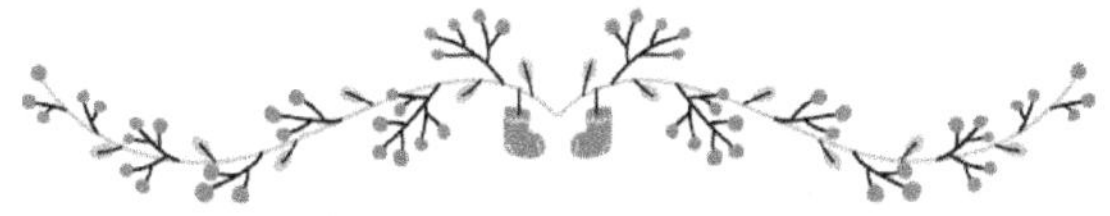

By connecting with nature, embracing seasonal traditions, and prioritizing balance, we can make the Yule season both magical and grounding. These mindful practices offer ways to embrace both solitude and togetherness, creating a holiday filled with meaning, calm, and connection.

This chapter invites readers to cherish the holiday season through mindful magic, fostering a deeper connection with Yule, themselves, and their communities.

Chapter 13

Navigating Holiday Stress with Magic and Mindfulness

The Yule season is a time for reflection and celebration, yet the holidays can also bring stress through busy schedules, family obligations, and social commitments. This chapter provides readers with mindful and magical practices to stay grounded, balanced, and connected to both personal traditions and the natural world, supporting a mindful, fulfilling holiday season.

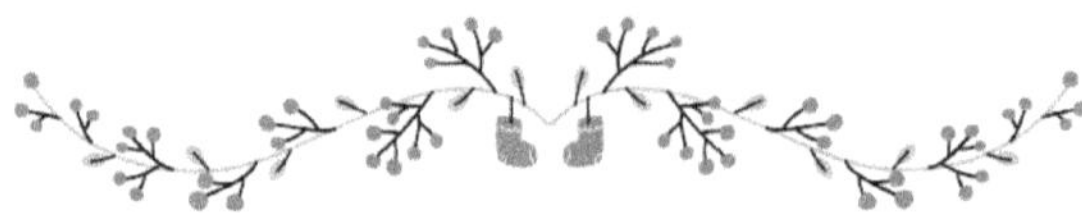

Embracing Seasonal Traditions with Mindful Practices

For many, Yule connects to ancient traditions that celebrate light, renewal, and the rhythms of nature. Integrating these mindful practices with Yule-inspired traditions can help readers feel more connected to the season's essence. Whether by lighting a candle to symbolize the return of the sun or journaling reflections on the past year, these practices bring a sense of timelessness, grounding, and alignment with the natural world.

Here are some ways to incorporate Yule traditions:

Winter Solstice Ritual: Honour the longest night of the year by lighting a candle, symbolizing the return of light. Spend a few minutes visualizing hopes for the coming year, using this ritual to let go of what no longer serves you and welcome new beginnings.

Nature Walks and Seasonal Décor: Collect winter greenery, pinecones, or seasonal herbs on a nature walk. Decorate your home with these natural elements, reconnecting with the outdoors and bringing a piece of the season inside.

Cultivating Balance in Giving and Receiving

The holidays are often centred around giving, yet a balanced exchange is crucial for meaningful connection. Mindfulness practices shared with loved ones create a space where giving and receiving can flow in harmony.

Consider these shared practices:

Guided Meditation with Loved Ones: Invite a friend or family member to join you in a simple meditation, such as the Embracing Light meditation from the previous chapter. Practicing together nurtures a mutual sense of warmth, peace, and connection.

Affirmations of Gratitude and Connection: Each morning, write one thing you're grateful to receive from a loved one and one way you can give back. Share these affirmations together, creating a mindful moment of appreciation for the relationships in your life.

Mindful Breaks and Boundaries

Amidst holiday gatherings, it's important to protect your well-being by finding time for mindful pauses and setting boundaries. These practices can help you feel empowered, balanced, and less pressured by social expectations.

Breathing Exercises and Mindfulness Pauses

When feeling overwhelmed, simple breathing exercises can create calm and centre you in the moment.

Three Deep Breaths: Take three long, slow breaths, releasing any tension with each exhale. This quick reset can be done anywhere, even during social events, to help you stay present.

4-7-8 Breath: Inhale for a count of 4, hold for 7, and exhale slowly for 8. This exercise is excellent before gatherings, helping ease social anxiety or post-event fatigue.

Setting Boundaries

The holidays bring an influx of activities, which can lead to emotional fatigue. By setting gentle boundaries, you make space for mindfulness and self-care.

Respect Your Own Limits: Practice saying "no" with compassion when you feel stretched too thin. Remember, protecting your well-being is an act of self-care.

Schedule 'You Time': Set aside specific times for yourself each week for reflection, hobbies, or relaxation. Consistent time to recharge will help you feel more present and energized when spending time with others.

Integrating Nature and the Seasons into Mindful Practices

Connecting with nature can deepen the effects of mindfulness practices, especially during the winter months when it's easy to feel disconnected from the natural world. Incorporate elements of the season, such as herbs or outdoor activities, into your practices to stay attuned to the rhythm of Yule.

Seasonal Herbs for Rituals: Use herbs like rosemary, cedar, and cinnamon in your rituals. These herbs evoke the warmth of the season and can be used in teas, baths, or incense to bring the essence of nature into your home.

Outdoor Meditation: If the weather permits, bundle up and meditate outdoors, appreciating the stillness of winter. Allow yourself to observe the beauty of nature in winter form, even if just for a few minutes, to feel more grounded and connected.

Magic for Balance and Peace

Adding simple, magical practices to your daily routine can create a shield of peace and protection, helping you maintain emotional balance through the season.

Protection and Grounding Spells

Simple Salt Protection Charm: Sprinkle a pinch of salt by doorways or windows, visualizing it as a barrier against stress and unwanted energies. This simple charm offers a sense of security and calm.

Grounding Stone Ritual: Carry a grounding stone like black tourmaline or smoky quartz with you. When feeling stressed, hold the stone, close your eyes, and imagine roots connecting you to the earth, stabilizing your energy.

Candle Spell for Peace

Light a white candle and focus on the flame, setting the intention to release stress and invite peace. Imagine the candlelight filling you with calm energy, gently melting away any tension.

Combating Emotional Fatigue from Social Expectations

The social demands of the holiday season can leave many feeling emotionally drained. To counter this, establish mindful habits to recharge and protect your energy.

Prioritize Self-Care: Make self-care a daily ritual, even if it's just a few minutes of meditation or a warm bath. Honour your need for rest and rejuvenation to prevent burnout.

Set Limits with Social Media and Technology: Consider taking breaks from social media or limiting screen time, especially if these activities increase feelings of stress or comparison.

Holiday Aromatherapy

Aromatherapy is a powerful tool for bringing balance, calm, and joy into your holiday season. Scents like pine, orange, and cinnamon are grounding and comforting, helping you connect with the warmth of the season.

Pine and Cedar for Grounding: Diffuse pine or cedar oils or place a drop on your wrist to root yourself in the present moment, perfect for winding down after busy days.

Lavender and Clove for Calm and Clarity: Use lavender to relax and clove for warmth and clarity, adding them to a bath or diffusing them to create a soothing atmosphere.

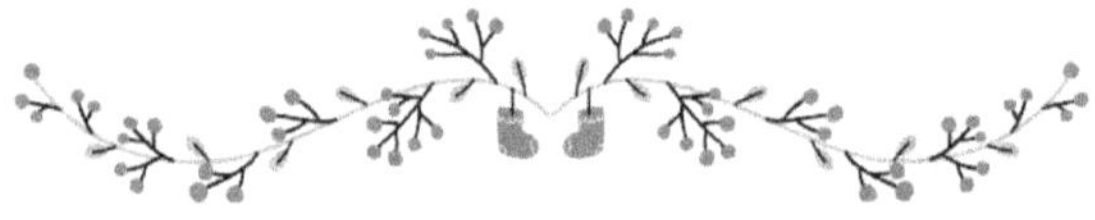

Incorporating these mindful and magical practices can help readers find joy and calm during the Yule season, connecting them to tradition, nature, and the spirit of giving and receiving. By embracing these practices, readers will welcome the holiday season with a sense of balance, self-compassion, and mindful magic.

Chapter 14

HONOURING THE END OF THE YEAR

As the Yule season and the calendar year come to a close, it's a natural time for reflection, gratitude, and release. This chapter guides readers through rituals and practices to acknowledge the passing year, let go of any lingering challenges, and begin envisioning their hopes for the New Year. By reconnecting with seasonal traditions, balancing giving and receiving, and embracing nature's cycles, readers can create a mindful close to the year and an inspired welcome to the next.

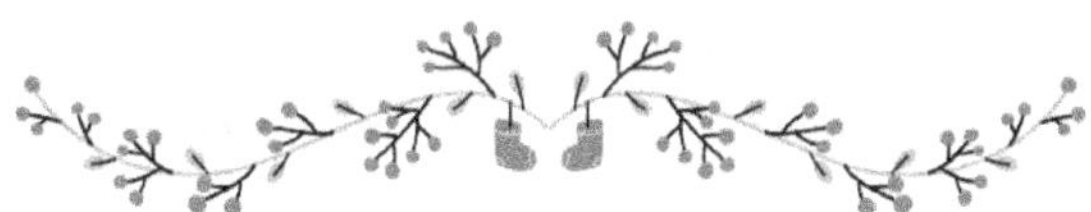

Reflection and Release

The end of the year is a powerful time for reflecting on personal growth, honouring lessons learned, and releasing any energy that no longer serves. Encourage readers to create a ritual space for contemplation, where they can gently let go of the past and make space for what's next.

Journaling Prompts for Reflection

Guide readers in reflecting on the past year with these journaling prompts, inviting them to consider moments of growth, resilience, and change:

What were the year's most significant moments for you?

- Think about milestones, challenges, and memorable experiences. What impact did they have on your personal journey?

What lessons did you learn, and how have they shaped you?

- Reflect on any insights, realizations, or skills you developed. How did these lessons change your perspective or approach?

What are you ready to release?

- Consider habits, fears, or emotional patterns you'd like to let go of. Imagine leaving them behind as you move forward into the New Year.

What are you most grateful for from this past year?

- Take a moment to honour moments of joy, support, and accomplishment. Allow these memories to bring a sense of gratitude and peace.

What intentions do you want to set for the upcoming year?

- Consider your dreams, goals, and aspirations. Think about how you can incorporate them into the New Year with purpose and hope.

Encourage readers to answer these prompts honestly and without judgment. These reflections serve as an opportunity to recognize the growth they've experienced and prepare for what's next.

Connecting to Seasonal Traditions

Yule, a season with roots in ancient winter celebrations, represents a time of introspection, renewal, and connection with the cycles of nature. By linking their reflections to traditional Yule customs—like lighting candles to honour the return of the sun, or crafting seasonal wreaths as symbols of growth and change—readers can feel more deeply connected to seasonal traditions. These small gestures create a bridge between past and present, inviting readers to celebrate the wisdom and warmth of this season in a way that feels meaningful.

Creating a Year's End Altar

Suggest creating a small Year's End altar to honour the past year and embody gratitude. This altar can serve as a visual representation of the journey, offering a chance to release any challenges and celebrate accomplishments.

Instructions for Creating a Year's End Altar:

Choose a Sacred Space: Select a small table, shelf, or corner where you can create a personal altar. Decorate it with a cloth, seasonal items, or colours that represent peace and reflection to you.

Gather Meaningful Items: Choose mementos that reflect the past year's journey: photos, symbols of achievements, or items connected to meaningful moments.

Incorporate natural elements, such as sprigs of rosemary or pine, to connect with the season's energy and create a grounded, earthy atmosphere.

Add Elements of Release: Place a small bowl or container to represent release. You can write any thoughts, worries, or memories you're ready to let go of on small pieces of paper, placing them in the bowl as a symbolic gesture.

Light Candles for Reflection: Light one or more candles, reflecting on each item on the altar. As you do, visualize yourself releasing any burdens and filling your heart with gratitude.

Express Gratitude and Close: After spending time at the altar, close the ritual by expressing gratitude to yourself, the year, and the journey you've taken. Leave the altar intact as a visual reminder of your growth and the light ahead.

Encourage readers to revisit this altar throughout the final days of the year, allowing it to serve as a point of focus for their intentions and reflections.

Balance Between Giving and Receiving

Holiday traditions often emphasize giving, but this can create an imbalance if self-care is neglected. Suggest to readers that these reflective practices can also be shared with loved ones, fostering a balance between giving and receiving. By inviting friends or family to join in activities like intention-setting, gratitude sharing, or altar creation, readers can create shared moments of mindfulness. This balance nurtures connection and makes space for both outward generosity and inward reflection.

Vision Board for the New Year

Creating a vision board is a powerful way to welcome the New Year with purpose. Encourage readers to craft a visual representation of their dreams, goals, and desires for the year ahead, setting a magical intention to guide them forward.

Step-by-Step Guide for Crafting a Vision Board

Set Your Intention: Before starting, spend a few moments in meditation, focusing on what you want to invite into your life. Think about the values, aspirations, and dreams that resonate most with you for the coming year.

Gather Materials: Gather a poster board, scissors, glue, magazines, and any art supplies for personalizing your board. You may also want to print or draw specific images, words, or symbols that capture your goals.

Find Inspiring Images and Words: Flip through magazines or search online for images that represent your dreams and intentions. Select words or phrases that embody qualities you want to bring into the New Year, such as "growth," "love," "adventure," or "peace."

Arrange Your Board: Arrange your images and words in a way that feels balanced and intentional. Some people like to place their core goals in the centre and surround them with complementary words and images, while others may prefer a collage style.

Affirm Your Vision: As you place each image, silently affirm its presence in your life. Visualize yourself experiencing the feelings associated with these dreams. Let yourself connect with a sense of joy, fulfilment, and possibility.

Display Your Vision Board: Place your vision board somewhere you'll see it often, such as near your altar, work desk, or bedroom. Each time you look at it, take a moment to focus on the feelings and intentions it represents.

The vision board will act as a reminder of the energy you want to carry into the New Year, helping readers stay focused and motivated as they move forward.

Managing Social Expectations and Preventing Burnout

As the season fills with gatherings and social obligations, emotional fatigue and burnout can arise. Encourage readers to prioritize self-care by setting boundaries and making time for their reflective practices, even amidst social commitments. Tips for staying balanced include:

Respect Your Own Limits: Remind readers that saying "no" to some invitations is an act of self-care.

Schedule Personal Time: Encourage readers to carve out moments for quiet reflection, hobbies, or simply unwinding, helping them stay grounded in their own needs.

Communicate with Kindness: Guide readers to set clear boundaries with compassion, ensuring they can enjoy both social and solitary moments without guilt.

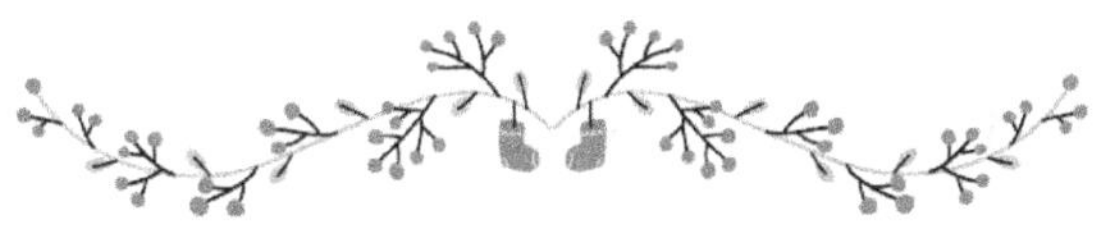

Through these practices of reflection, connection, and mindfulness, readers can honour the end of the year with intention and magic, embracing closure and possibility as they turn the page to a new year.

Chapter 15

Holiday Rituals and Spells for Balance and Joy

The holiday season is a time of enchantment, filled with moments of reflection, gratitude, and anticipation. As we navigate the darkest days of winter, we can turn to rituals and spells to bring balance, joy, and a sense of renewal into our lives. This chapter offers a collection of simple yet powerful rituals that align with the energies of the lunar phases, the New Year, and the magic of Yule. Embrace these practices to deepen your connection to the season, reconnect with nature and time-honoured traditions, and create a harmonious holiday experience filled with balance and joy.

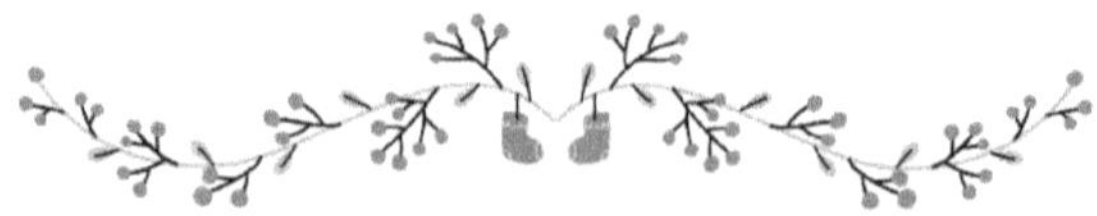

Full Moon and New Moon Winter Rituals

The lunar cycles hold potent energy that can be harnessed through mindful rituals. During the holiday season, the Full Moon and New Moon provide unique opportunities for release, manifestation, and gratitude.

Full Moon Ritual: Embracing Release and Gratitude

The Full Moon is a time of culmination and illumination, making it an ideal moment to release what no longer serves you and express gratitude for the blessings in your life.

Materials Needed:

- A white candle

- A piece of paper and a pen

- A small bowl of water

- Crystals (optional, such as moonstone or clear quartz)

Ritual Steps:

1. Find a quiet space where you won't be disturbed. Light the white candle to symbolize the Full Moon's light.

2. Take a few deep breaths and centre yourself. Reflect on the past month and identify any negative thoughts, habits, or emotions you wish to release.

3. Write down what you want to let go of on the paper, visualizing these things leaving your life.

4. Hold the paper and say, "Under the light of the Full Moon, I release these burdens and make space for new blessings."

5. Burn the paper (safely, using a fireproof container) or place it in the bowl of water to symbolize the release of these energies.

6. Express gratitude for the positive aspects of your life. Hold the crystals (if using) and thank the universe for your blessings.

7. Close the ritual by extinguishing the candle and feeling the sense of release and renewal.

New Moon Ritual: Manifesting Intentions

The New Moon is a time of new beginnings and setting intentions. This ritual focuses on manifesting your desires and planting the seeds for future growth.

Materials Needed:

- A black or dark-coloured candle

- A piece of paper and a pen

- A small bowl of earth or sand

- Seeds (optional, such as sunflower or marigold seeds)

Ritual Steps:

1. Find a quiet space where you won't be disturbed. Light the black candle to symbolize the New Moon's hidden potential.

2. Reflect on your goals and desires for the coming month and year.

3. Write your intentions, using specific and positive language.

4. Hold the paper and say, "Under the darkness of the New Moon, I plant the seeds of my intentions. May they grow and flourish."

5. Place the paper in the bowl of earth or sand, symbolizing the planting of your intentions. If using seeds, plant them in the bowl as well.

6. Close the ritual by extinguishing the candle and feeling the sense of potential and new beginnings.

Blessing the Home for the New Year

As the New Year approaches, it's a perfect time to purify and bless your home, setting fresh intentions while releasing the old. This ritual helps create a sacred space filled with positive energy.

Materials Needed:

- A smudge stick (such as sage) or incense

- A bowl of water with a pinch of salt

- A white candle

- A small bell or chime

- A piece of paper and a pen

Ritual Steps:

1. Begin by opening the windows to allow fresh air to circulate. Light the smudge stick or incense and walk through your home, allowing the smoke to cleanse each room. Visualize any negative energy being released.

2. Place the bowl of water with salt in the centre of your living space. Light the white candle next to it.

3. Dip your fingers into the water and sprinkle it around the room, saying, "I cleanse this space of all negativity. May it be filled with light and positivity."

4. Ring the bell or chime in each room, inviting positive energy with sound.

5. Write your intentions for the New Year. Be clear and specific about what you wish to welcome.

6. Hold the paper and say, "I bless this home with love, peace, and prosperity. May it be a sanctuary of joy and harmony."

7. Place the paper in a special place, such as your altar or a favourite spot, letting the candle burn for a while before extinguishing it.

Candle Magic for Yule Wishes

Candle magic is a simple yet powerful way to focus your intentions and send them into the universe. This Yule candle ritual helps you express gratitude for the past year and set intentions for the next.

Materials Needed:

- A red, green, or white candle (or all three)

- A piece of paper and a pen

- A fireproof container

- Herbs or oils (optional, such as rosemary, cinnamon, or frankincense)

Ritual Steps:

1. Find a quiet space where you won't be disturbed. If using herbs or oils, anoint the candle(s) with them to enhance the ritual's energy.

2. Light the candle(s) and centre yourself. Reflect on the past year and the experiences, lessons, and blessings it brought.

3. Write your wishes and intentions for the coming year. Be specific and positive.

4. Hold the paper and say, "With this candle's light, I express my gratitude for the past year and set my intentions for the next. May my wishes come true."

5. Carefully burn the paper in the fireproof container, visualizing your intentions being carried into the universe with the candle's flame.

6. Close the ritual by allowing the candle(s) to burn for a while before extinguishing them.

1. Embracing Yule's Connection to Nature and Traditions

Incorporate seasonal herbs, flowers, or outdoor settings into these rituals to deepen your connection to Yule traditions and the natural world. Adding rosemary, holly, or pine branches can create a sacred atmosphere filled with winter's unique aromas, bringing the energy of the season to your rituals.

Fostering Balance Through Shared Rituals

Consider sharing these rituals with loved ones as a way to create a balance of giving and receiving during Yule. Inviting others into these practices fosters connection and joy, allowing you to give the gift of ritual while opening yourself to receive their presence and support in return.

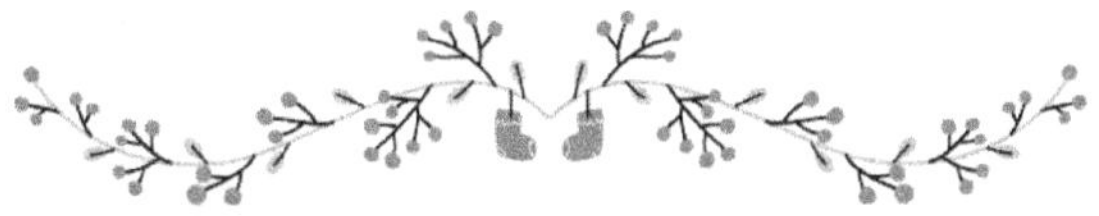

The holiday season often brings social expectations and obligations that can lead to emotional fatigue. To make time for these rituals amidst your commitments, consider setting gentle boundaries, prioritizing your well-being, and carving out sacred time for mindfulness and self-care.

By incorporating these holiday rituals and spells into your celebrations, you can bring balance, joy, and a deeper connection to the season. Embrace the magic of winter and let it guide you toward a harmonious and fulfilling holiday experience.

Chapter 16

INTENTION-DRIVEN GIFTS FOR A MAGICAL HOLIDAY

The art of gift-giving takes on a deeper meaning when infused with intention, care, and thoughtfulness. Rather than opting for mass-produced presents, consider creating personalized, intention-driven gifts that resonate with the recipient and foster a sense of connection. The act of creating and giving these unique, meaningful gifts can be a powerful tool to support mental health during the holiday season, offering a sense of purpose and joy through both the making and the giving.

Mental Health Benefits of Intentional Gift-Giving

For many, the holiday season can bring emotional fatigue and feelings of disconnect. Creating handmade, intentional gifts not only brings joy to others, but also provides the giver with a sense of accomplishment and purpose. The focus shifts from holiday stress to the joy of crafting something meaningful, supporting mental health by offering an outlet for creativity and connection.

Personalized Sachets and Charm Bags

Sachets and charm bags are small but powerful tokens of protection, love, and good luck. Filled with carefully chosen herbs, crystals, and written intentions, they make heartfelt and magical gifts that connect us to seasonal and traditional practices.

- Materials Needed:

- Small fabric bags or pouches

- Dried herbs (e.g., lavender, rosemary, chamomile)

- Small crystals (e.g., amethyst, rose quartz, clear quartz)

- Small pieces of paper and a pen

- Ribbon or string

Instructions:

1. Choose the Purpose: Decide on the purpose of your sachet or charm bag (e.g., protection, love, good luck) and select corresponding herbs and crystals.

2. Set the Intention: Write a short intention or affirmation on a piece of paper, fold it, and place it inside the bag.

3. Infuse with Care: Add the dried herbs and crystals to the bag, visualizing your intention being infused into each item.

4. Present with Meaning: Gift the sachet with a note explaining its purpose and the intention behind it.

These simple yet powerful gifts can be a meaningful way to incorporate Yule symbols, like herbs and natural materials, allowing you to stay connected with traditional practices.

Crafting Intention Candles

Creating candles with intention is a wonderful way to impart blessings, light, and love. The soothing ritual of candle-making fosters a meditative atmosphere, helping you unwind and reconnect with the season.

Materials Needed:

- Small candle molds or containers

- Wax (e.g., soy wax, beeswax)

- Wicks

- Essential oils (e.g., lavender, rosemary, peppermint)

- Herbs or dried flowers (optional)

- Small crystals (optional)

Instructions:

1. Melt the wax in a double boiler until it reaches a liquid state.

2. Add essential oils to the melted wax, stirring gently. Optional: add herbs or dried flowers for added magic.

3. Place the wick in the centre of the mold or container and pour the wax around it.

4. Allow the candle to cool and solidify. Once set, add small crystals for additional intention.

Intention candles are a simple, magical way to share your light and love, as well as an invitation to slow down and embrace the season's serenity.

Potions, Infusions, and Herbal Remedies

Handmade herbal remedies offer a personal touch, and using natural, seasonal ingredients fosters a sense of connection with nature.

Soothing Tea Blend

- 1 part dried chamomile

- 1 part dried lavender

- 1 part dried lemon balm

Instructions: Mix the herbs, then fill small tea bags or jars. Include a note: "Steep 1-2 teaspoons in hot water for 5-10 minutes. Enjoy a peaceful moment."

Herbal Bath Salts

- 1 cup Epsom salt

- ½ cup sea salt

- ½ cup baking soda

- Dried rose petals

- Essential oil (e.g., lavender, eucalyptus)

Instructions: Combine the salts and baking soda, add essential oil and rose petals, and package. Include a note: "Add a handful to a warm bath. Relax and let the healing energy embrace you."

By using nature's seasonal ingredients, these gifts encourage a grounding connection to the earth.

Setting Boundaries and Prioritizing Self-Care

While crafting meaningful gifts can be a soothing ritual, it's important to set boundaries and prioritize self-care. The pressure to meet holiday expectations can lead to burnout, so ensure that you don't over-commit. Approach the gift-making process as a journey rather than a task and take breaks when needed. Enjoying the creation process and setting manageable limits are essential steps to ensure that your energy remains balanced.

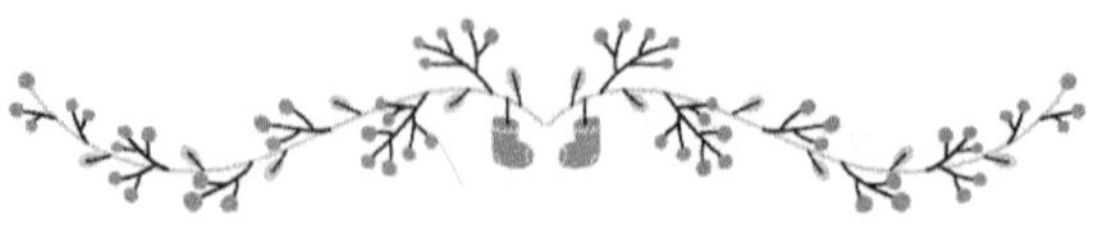

As the holiday season fades, remember that the principles of mindful magic can continue to guide you all year long. Reflect on the growth, balance, and peace you have cultivated, and consider seasonal rituals, daily mindfulness practices, and intentional living to keep these values alive throughout the year.

Chapter 17

CARRYING THE SPIRIT OF THE CHRISTMAS WITCH FORWARD

As the holiday season wraps up and a fresh year begins, the lessons and magic from this time don't need to end. In this final chapter, we'll explore ways to carry forward the spirit of the Christmas Witch—rooted in kindness, mindfulness, and self-care—throughout the year. By cultivating ongoing practices and creating personal traditions, readers can weave the spirit of Yule into their lives, helping them feel grounded and connected all year long.

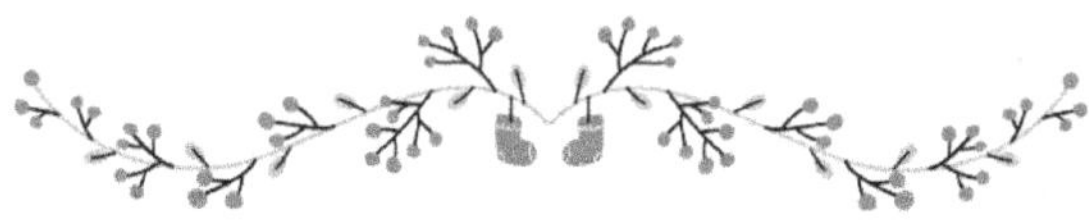

Supporting Mental Health Beyond the Holidays

The holidays can be a challenging time, with increased social pressures and a focus on festivities that may feel overwhelming. Continuing self-care practices throughout the year can help support mental well-being beyond this season. Regular grounding exercises, mindfulness practices, and self-compassion can ease stress and provide resilience against the highs and lows of life. These small moments of care, carried forward from Yule, offer essential tools for managing mental health struggles not just during the holidays, but every day.

Continuing Self-Care into the New Year

The self-care routines developed over the Yule season don't have to be limited to the holidays. These practices can become part of everyday life, providing grounding, resilience, and joy long after the decorations are put away.

Tips for Maintaining Mindfulness and Magic Beyond the Holiday Season

Monthly Rituals: Choose a day each month, such as the new or full moon, to pause and check in with yourself. Use this time to meditate, journal, or set intentions. Reflect on what's working well in your life and where you may need to adjust, staying mindful of your well-being.

Seasonal Gratitude: Practice gratitude at the start of each season. Create a simple ritual to celebrate the arrival of spring, summer, fall, and winter, acknowledging the cyclical nature of time and the changing energies around you.

Daily Mindful Moments: Dedicate a few minutes each morning to grounding yourself with affirmations or breathing exercises. Use these moments to centre yourself and set the tone for your day, carrying forward the spirit of self-compassion and calm cultivated during the Yule season.

Weekly Self-Care Check-In: Reserve a bit of time each week to assess your emotional and physical needs. Create a small ritual to honour your body and spirit, such as a warm bath, tea ceremony, or quiet journaling session. This regular commitment to self-care can help you stay balanced and mindful year-round.

Staying Connected to Seasonal Traditions

Incorporating traditional Yule practices can deepen your connection to the seasonal rhythms and provide continuity with nature. Consider lighting candles to honour the return of light during the winter season or incorporating greenery, like pine and holly, to bring nature indoors. Even small gestures, like setting aside time to reflect on the shifting seasons, help keep you grounded in the traditions of Yule throughout the year.

Ideas for Nature-Based Traditions and Practices

Incorporate Seasonal Herbs in Rituals: Embrace nature's rhythms by using seasonal herbs and flowers in your rituals. In winter, use evergreen sprigs; in spring, try lavender or rosemary. Infuse them in teas, bath salts, or candles to honour each season's unique energy.

Create a Seasonal Altar or Space: Decorate a small space in your home to honour each season. Use natural elements like stones, leaves, or flowers to represent the cycles of growth, rest, and renewal that come with each change in nature.

Setting Boundaries Amidst Social Expectations

The holiday season often brings social obligations, which can lead to emotional fatigue and burnout. Prioritizing self-care and mindfulness practices throughout the year, even during busy times, is essential. Setting clear boundaries and creating space for rest allows you to approach obligations without feeling overwhelmed. By honouring your need for solitude or quiet, you protect your energy and well-being.

Tips for Balancing Social Obligations with Self-Care

Schedule Alone Time: Don't be afraid to carve out restful time for yourself amidst gatherings or social activities. A short walk, quiet reading, or mindful breathing can help you recharge.

Practice Saying No: Honour your limits and remember that declining certain social invitations is okay. A polite "no, thank you" can prevent burnout and create space for the moments that nourish you.

Use Mindfulness as a Centreing Tool: Before any social engagement, take a moment to ground yourself with a few deep breaths or an affirmation. These small practices help you feel connected to yourself, bringing calm and presence into social interactions.

Creating a Personal Holiday Legacy

As you carry forward the spirit of the Christmas Witch, consider building a legacy of holiday traditions that resonates with your beliefs and values. Whether through rituals, gatherings, or symbolic acts, these traditions can become meaningful ways to honour the magic and wisdom of Yule for years to come.

Inspire Readers to Cultivate Holiday Traditions that Resonate Personally and Spiritually

Define Your Core Values: Reflect on what matters to you during the holiday season: kindness, family, reflection, or renewal. Allow these core values to guide your holiday traditions, ensuring that your celebrations align with your spirit and beliefs.

Create a Tradition of Giving: Honour the giving spirit of the Christmas Witch by incorporating acts of kindness into your annual holiday plans. This could include making donations to charities, helping in community projects, or organizing a small Yule exchange with handmade gifts to spread joy and connection.

Keep a Holiday Grimoire: Document each year's holiday season in a special grimoire or journal. Write rituals, reflections, recipes, and memories. Over time, this grimoire will become a treasured collection of your personal traditions, filled with the wisdom and warmth of each passing season.

Host an Annual Winter Gathering: Establish an annual gathering of friends or family to celebrate Yule. It could be a simple candle-lit dinner, a storytelling evening, or a cozy potluck. Use this gathering to nurture bonds and honour the season's themes of light, warmth, and unity.

Set an Annual Intention Ceremony: At the end of each year, hold an intention-setting ritual to welcome the New Year. Light a candle, meditate on your hopes, and write your intentions. Seal them in a small envelope or jar to revisit at the year's end, allowing this tradition to support your journey forward with purpose.

Create a Winter Nature Walk Tradition: Plan an annual nature walk or hike to honour the season's beauty. Whether alone or with loved ones, spend time in the winter landscape, embracing the peaceful magic of the natural world as a grounding tradition each year.

Embody the Christmas Witch's Spirit of Kindness Year-Round

Commit to regular acts of kindness, not just during Yule but throughout the year. Small, thoughtful gestures—such as a handwritten note, a spontaneous phone call, or a little gift—can help cultivate the Christmas Witch's nurturing energy in everyday life.

The journey of the Christmas Witch is one of kindness, magic, and self-discovery. By carrying these practices forward, you embrace the spirit of the Christmas Witch not only as a holiday archetype but as a personal symbol of compassion and wisdom that you can turn to all year long.

As you continue these practices, remember that the magic of the Christmas Witch is not limited to Yule but lives within you, waiting to inspire, guide, and nurture you as you move through the seasons of life. May each day bring you closer to yourself. Each season reminds you of the magic in the world, and each year deepens your understanding of the spirit of Yule.

Blessings of peace, joy, and magic to carry with you always.

Conclusion

CARRYING FORWARD THE SPIRIT OF MINDFUL MAGIC

As the final notes of the holiday season begin to fade and we transition into the new year, it's essential to remember that the principles of mindful magic we've explored aren't confined to the festive period alone. The tranquillity, intention, and renewal that you've cultivated during Yule and the winter solstice can become a consistent, guiding force throughout the year.

Reflecting on Your Journey

As you reflect on the practices and rituals you've embraced, take a moment to acknowledge the growth, balance, and peace you've brought into your life. Each breath of mindfulness, each act of self-care, each intentional spell has contributed to a richer, more connected experience of the season. By honouring these moments, you anchor the wisdom and serenity of Yule within yourself.

Integrating Mindful Magic Year-Round

The tools and techniques of mindful magic are not reserved for the winter months; they are lifelong companions that can help you navigate all seasons with grace and intention. Here are a few ways to continue this journey:

Seasonal Rituals: As each season turns, create rituals that honour the energies of spring, summer, and autumn, just as you have done with Yule. Whether it's planting intentions in the spring, basking in the sun's vitality in the summer, or harvesting gratitude in the autumn, let the cycles of nature guide your practice.

Daily Mindfulness: Incorporate simple mindfulness practices into your daily routine. A few minutes of meditation, deep breathing, or a mindful walk can ground you and keep you connected to the present moment.

Self-Care Practices: Continue to prioritize your well-being with regular self-care rituals. Whether it's a soothing bath, journaling, or spending time in nature, these practices nourish your spirit and maintain your emotional balance.

Intentional Living: Approach each day with the same intentionality you've brought to your holiday rituals. Set daily or weekly intentions, practice gratitude, and stay mindful of your energy and needs.

Embracing the Lessons of the Season

The holiday season has provided a unique opportunity to explore the depths of mindful magic. Carry forward the lessons of balance, compassion, and self-awareness you've gained. Let them shape your interactions, decisions, and dreams throughout the year.

A Year of Continuous Growth

Your journey of mindful magic and holiday healing is ongoing. With each passing year, you have the opportunity to deepen your practice, refine your rituals, and enhance your connection to the natural world and your inner self. Embrace the perpetual cycle of growth, knowing that each season brings its own magic and wisdom.

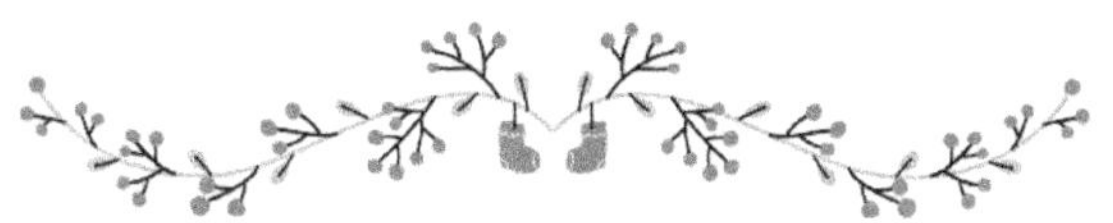

In closing, remember that the essence of the Christmas Witch and the magic of Yule lie within you. By integrating mindfulness and witchcraft into your daily life, you can create a sanctuary of peace, balance, and purpose that extends beyond the holiday season. May your journey be filled with light, love, and the enduring magic of mindful intention.

Blessings of joy and serenity as you carry the spirit of mindful magic forward.

Thank you

Thank You for Reading!

Thank you for joining me on this journey—I'm so grateful for your time and support! Your feedback means a lot to me, and hearing from readers is one of the best parts of being an author. If you enjoyed the book, I'd love it if you could take a moment to share your thoughts in a review on Amazon. Your reviews help other readers discover my work, and I appreciate every word.

If you'd like to reach out directly, feel free to contact me at Kelsey.Pearce.Grit@gmail.com. I'd be delighted to hear from you!

With heartfelt thanks,

Kelsey

Also by Kelsey Pearce

Mindful Magic Series:

Mindful Magic: A Guide to Modern Witchcraft for Mental Wellness &
Self-Care ISBN 978-1738290574

A beginners guide to magic and intention. This book takes a inclusive and accessible approach to magic encouraging anyone to build their our practice. Learn how to create your own spells or leverage the twenty-five premade spells.

Mindful Magic for The Kitchen Witch: Crafting Nourishment and
Self-Care Through Recipes and Rituals ISBN 978-1738290598

With simple recipes and practical insights, this book invites you to create meals that not only nourish the body but uplift the spirit. Perfect for beginner and seasoned kitchen witches alike, this guide brings magic to your daily rituals and helps you cultivate a kitchen that's brimming with intention, love, and powerful energy. Over thirty recipes leveraging easily accessible ingredients with magical properties included.

Spell Crafting: Witchcraft resource that includes reference material for
crystals, herbs, lunar magic, and more. ISBN 978-1738290567

Build your own Book of Shadows or Grimoire with these easy templates and reference material.

Resiliency and Gratitude Series:

Grateful Grit: Building Resilience Through Gratitude   ISBN 978-1738290529

Learn how gratitude in the face of adversity can help build resilience and your growth mindset.

Happiness for the Senses: Mindful Sensory Experience: Taste, Touch, Sight, Smell, Sound ISBN 978-1738290505

Learn how to engage all of your senses to find happiness and mindfulness.

Bonus Craft

T-SHIRT YARN

Create your own T-shirt yarn for projects. A man's XL should create at least 28 yards (25.6 m) or more if knotting on the additional top portions.

01.

Cut through both layers of the T-Shirt from arm pit to arm pit.

02.

Rotate the T-shirt 90°

03.

Cut the strips about 1.5" or 3.8 cm, stopping about 2" or 5 cm from the top fold.

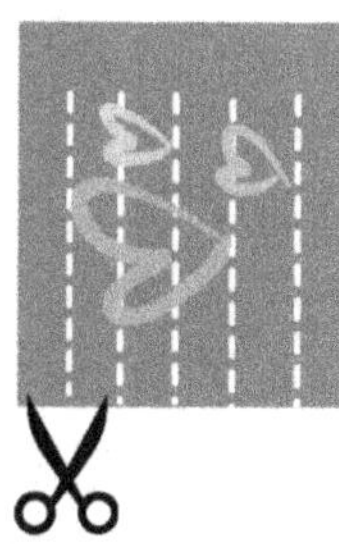

04.

Work on the top portion (side) of the T-shirt. Cut from the outside to the upper strip. Cut from lower cut diagonally to the upper strip.

05.

Gently tug and stretch the T-Shirt yarn lengthwise and it will curl on itself. Roll into a ball.

OPTIONAL

Create strips with the remaining T-shirt attaching with a double slip knot pulled tight.

Upcycled T-Shirt Candle Holder

Supplies:

- Old T-shirt cut into strips (see instructions)
- Empty glass jar
- Tea light candle or LED light.

Instructions:

- Wrap the yarn around the outside of a jar, leaving some gaps to let light through
- Tie it off at the top.
- Place a tea light or LED candle

Select Colours For Magical Intention

- White: Purity, peace, and new beginnings.
- Green: Growth, renewal, and prosperity.
- Red: Strength, courage, and passion.
- Blue: Calm, communication, and clarity.

Wrap with Intention: envision weaving intent for the new year as you wrap the yarn around the jar.